Special Events Programs in School Library Media Centers

Greenwood Professional Guides in School Librarianship

School Library Media Centers in the 21st Century: Changes and Challenges
Kathleen W. Craver

Developing a Vision: Strategic Planning and the Library Media Specialist
John D. Crowley

Serving Special Needs Students in the School Library Media Center
Caren L. Wesson and Margaret J. Keefe, editors

Collaborations for Literacy: Creating an Integrated Language Arts Program for Middle Schools
Rochelle B. Senator

How to Teach about American Indians: A Guide for the School Library Media Specialist
Karen D. Harvey with Lisa D. Harjo and Lynda Welborn

100 Research Topic Guides for Students
Barbara Wood Borne

Special Events Programs in School Library Media Centers
A Guide to Making Them Work

MARCIA TROTTA

Greenwood Professional Guides in School Librarianship
Harriet Selverstone, Series Adviser

GREENWOOD PRESS
Westport, Connecticut • London

Library of Congress Cataloging-in-Publication Data

Trotta, Marcia.
    Special events programs in school library media centers : a guide to making them work / Marcia Trotta.
        p. cm. — (Greenwood professional guides in school librarianship, ISSN 1074–150X)
    Includes bibliographical references and index.
    ISBN 0–313–29190–X (alk. paper)
    1. School libraries—Activity programs—United States. I. Title. II. Series.
    Z675.S3T73   1997
    027.8—dc20   96–22009

British Library Cataloguing in Publication Data is available.

Copyright © 1997 by Marcia Trotta

All rights reserved. No portion of this book may be reproduced, by any process or technique, without the express written consent of the publisher.

Library of Congress Catalog Card Number: 96–22009
ISBN: 0–313–29190–X
ISSN: 1074–150X

First published in 1997

Greenwood Press, 88 Post Road West, Westport, CT 06881
An imprint of Greenwood Publishing Group, Inc.

Printed in the United States of America

The paper used in this book complies with the Permanent Paper Standard issued by the National Information Standards Organization (Z39.48–1984).

10 9 8 7 6 5 4 3 2 1

To Mom and Dad,
who taught me the value
of a good education

Contents

Introduction		1
1	The Need for Special Events as a Part of the Reading Program	9
2	On Your Mark, Get Set, Program! Developing Special Events Programs Relevant to the Curriculum	17
3	Developing Partnerships to Support Special Events Programs	43
4	Raising Community Support for and Awareness of the Media Center and Its Programs	49
5	Personnel Training and Strategies	57
6	Developing Promotional Materials for Special Events	67
7	Keys to Making Programs Successful	79
8	Programs on a Shoestring: Learning to Budget and Raise Funds for Special Events Programs	93
9	Resources	99
Index		113

Special Events Programs in School Library Media Centers

Introduction

Any educator would agree that children are the most important facet of any school. They are the ones who are there to learn (even though, as adults, we learn a great deal from them!). We are there to help them develop the ability to think clearly, creatively, and critically. Educators might choose different things as necessities to have available to students: some would list the curriculum, others facilities or equipment, and still others the professional staff. This book stresses the vital role of the school library media center and the media specialist for resource-based learning. From kindergarten through high school, the school library media center should be a conduit through which much learning takes place. It is the one component of a school that is able to provide the framework for interdisciplinary instruction. Through the school library media center, instructors are best able to integrate information and technology skills into curriculum objectives. Special events hosted by the school library media center can provide a different way to meet this goal.

All too often, nonlibrarians feel that the media center is a frill that is nice to have but not essential. The American Library Association's *Information Power* (1989) defines the mission of the school library media center very clearly: its role is to ensure that all students and staff become effective users of ideas and information.[1] What could be more important in the information age? This role is significantly different from the media center's original function as a repository for curriculum support materials. Today's school library is information power because of its ability to effectively match the right information to the right individual at the right time. To be effective, it is critical that the school library media program be recognized as a central focus in the learning process by administrators, teachers, and students. School media centers provide a variety of information in a variety of formats. The activities and programs facilitate the use of information. The school system operates for the benefit of children, in an environment that includes a number of adults in various roles: parents, teachers, and other support staff. School media centers must relate to those who work with children as well. Very often, an adult is the intermediary through which the school library serves the child. By the very nature of its content, the school library media center has the potential for developing a love of learning in students. It is the responsibility of the media specialist to make sure the facility is fully understood by all who will benefit from its use. Take the time to recognize this role, and accept it as your responsibility. Then use special events programs as tools to help people gain an appreciation of the resources of the media center.

DEFINING THE ROLE OF THE MEDIA CENTER

This wide-ranging role for the school library media center is consistent with the educational philosophy of the American Association of School Librarians (AASL). Its position statement recommends that the library media program be fully integrated into the educational program of the district. AASL notes that such integration "strengthens the teaching/learning process so that students can develop the vital skills necessary to locate, analyze, evaluate, interpret and communicate ideas and information."[2] Special events are a creative way of meeting this standard.

Partnerships mean that everyone involved takes responsibility. This is another factor that generates effective learning. Children, like adults, have different learning styles, and the partnerships developed by the school library media center are one strategy for meeting this learning challenge. The students' intellectual development is at stake, not for a day or a school year, but for a lifetime, since processing information is a critical life skill. A school library media program can help students and their parents cope with the information explosion. Much research cites resource-based learning as one of the most effective tools available to help students develop the ability to think clearly, to solve problems, and to communicate effectively. The media center is resource-based, and thus its importance in the learning process must not be undervalued.[3]

To be an effective partner in learning, the school library media center must provide a variety of appropriate materials in all of the available formats. All of these materials are crucial in helping students learn to think clearly through their own firsthand perceptions and through interpretation. Special events are one way of presenting information. Programs are actually nonprint resources. Ideally, the media center will be adequately funded in order to provide enough up-to-date, quality materials in a variety of formats, and have enough qualified staff to assist the students in the use of these materials. Special events such as storytelling, booktalks, author visits, and dramatic play give students the opportunity to practice their thinking skills and enhance their learning experience. A rich learning tapestry can be created by cooperative efforts. Partnerships between the school library media specialist and the other personnel responsible for the students' learning are necessary to achieve success in integrating information in all learning situations. Mutual understanding of each other's roles is vital to the success of the partnership; indeed, special events can be planned around this need as well as around the students' needs.

However, before attempting to offer special events, library media specialists must develop both a comfort level with their job, and the confidence to share information about their role with others. The specialist's role should be clearly defined in a mission statement, which must be harmonious with the mission statement of the school. The mission statement provides the basic foundation for goal setting, for allocation of resources, and for measuring the impact that these practices will have on the students' learning. The media specialist should take the responsibility of making sure that all students have equal access to information. The media center should provide an environment in which children are able to ask any questions they want without fear of looking foolish, and with the security of knowing that they can learn wherever they can find facts.

Before a mission statement is set down in writing, the school library media center's role within the school community must be clearly established. Information provision calls for active participation on the part of the provider and the user, which, coincidentally, works well with the natural curiosity of youth. The oral, written, and thinking skills that we expect children to learn from this experience are relevant. When they are reinforced, they then become part of the child's ability to transfer the skills to future applications.

No two library media centers are the same, even within the same school system. Different environments, experiences, cultural backgrounds, and resources should be reflected in the mission statement. A few basics, however, can be applied across the board. Three common goals are often found in school library media programs. The first is to help maintain reading skills through the provision of print materials. The school library media program can combat functional illiteracy. The problem of students graduating from high school without literacy skills has been in the news regularly in recent years. The media center can help alleviate this problem by helping students to develop adequate comprehension, writing, and numeric skills. For a student who may be struggling with these basic life skills in the classroom, the school library media environment and the special programs it offers may be the answer. The second goal is to serve as an introduction to the use of nonprint materials. Not all children have access to the electronic media and software that are becoming more and more basic in everyday life. The school library media center can be viewed as a laboratory in this respect for many, and special events programs might be a useful way to introduce them. The third goal is to give learners guidance in the selection of appropriate print and nonprint materials for individual use. With the enormous amount of information available, children and adults need the assistance of professionals equipped to focus on just the right information. Special events programs are tools to provide this focus.[4]

Part of our public responsibility in education is to establish programs and provide adequate funding to allow the school library media program to meet its role. The school media program is concerned with whole learning, the ability to develop relationships that link developed concepts. Unit or theme approaches that cut across the boundaries of different disciplines are not effective unless they become resources that stimulate learning. This is the area in which the school media specialist's role is vital, since the media center provides the resource opportunities that allow this learning to take place. This is another reason why special events work so well.

PLANNING

The school library media specialist must take the time to define the center's goals within the educational structure. First and foremost, the underlying attitude and the overall atmosphere of the media center set the tone for the development of interdepartmental relationships within the school community. Ultimately, this will be the key to the success of the school library media program. The school media program must have goals that will help the students move forward in their educational process so that they will be able to adapt to the changing environment of the twenty-first century.

The process of goal setting is recognized as an essential management responsibility. *America 2000* represents the best thinking on the part of our nation for educational reform. Prepared in 1991 as a result of the National Education Strategy Meeting, the direction of this document is to develop and implement higher academic standards in science, math, history, English, geography, foreign languages, and the arts. The school library media center can be instrumental in providing the foundation and the enhancement activities for these programs. The document encourages partnerships among parents, educators, businesspeople, and, in fact, all citizens. Special events programs can provide a means for these people to get involved in education and to help improve the quality of students' educational experiences. Therefore, it is appropriate that the goals set down by an individual school media center reflect the thinking of the plan, and serve as benchmarks in evaluating the strengths and weaknesses of the programs.[5]

How this can be achieved becomes clearer if we take a look at each of the goals. The first goal addresses school readiness. School media centers in the elementary schools can reach out to the parents of preschoolers in their community. They can work in coordination with the public library to provide informational programs for parents on what they can do at home to help prepare their children for their school years. School media centers can invite families to participate in appropriate special events, for example, hearing an illustrator of children's picture books speak. This type of activity can also help with another goal—getting parents involved in their children's education.

By its very nature, the school library media center has the ability to foster students' interest in their work, of vital importance in the effort to increase the national rate of graduation to 90 percent, as expressed in *America 2000*. The school library media center environment works to the benefit of the school. The teaching methods utilized by the school media specialist are different from classroom routines. Interdisciplinary enhancements can be viewed as tools to increase competency across the various disciplines and to ensure that students are being prepared to take a responsible role in society. The school library media center can be a leader in creating an atmosphere that encourages adult literacy and lifelong learning. One of its most far-reaching goals is that every American will be literate and will possess the knowledge and skills necessary to compete in a global economy, and to exercise the rights and responsibilities of citizenship. Creating a lifelong reading habit through special events programs in the school library media center *is* a significant contribution to America's future.

Once steps have been taken to clarify all the roles that the various participants in a community will play, one can proceed with the cooperative planning process. School principals have an important function in this process because their job already involves harmonizing the various roles of different personnel. The principal is the catalyst for planning, contributing enthusiasm that will help define the qualitative as well as quantitative goals that should be part of the school library media program. The principal is the person who oversees the continued professional development of the staff and can ensure that the staff have the same understanding of curriculum theory, learning theory, child development, and educational philosophy. Through this process, the staff will have the opportunity to explore each other's expertise and become familiar with changes in the disciplines as they occur.

The primary mission of schools everywhere is to provide a learning environment for students, and the media center should be providing the information necessary to enhance these learning experiences. The underlying principle of all library services is that the library (media center) is most effective when it responds to the needs to the community. The goals that a school sets in addition to its primary mission must reflect the uniqueness of that particular school. The quality of the program is dependent on responding to particular needs. The needs identification process must be repeated on a regular basis, to ensure that library programs continue to meet the community's needs.

Many documents are available to help with the planning process, including materials published by the American Library Association and the American Association of School Librarians. (See Chapter 9 for citations.) Here I simply wish to emphasize a few guiding principles. We must be acutely aware of our audience. We must be able to judge the behavior and the skills of those who are to be served. Planning is most successful when it targets particular "market segments" and identifies specific needs. These are essentials that must be considered before one begins the process of offering special programs.

A variety of different methods can be used to gather background materials and ideas that will provide a clear picture of the needs of the specialized market (audience). The use of focus groups is one method. Small groups can be chosen to provide input on topics of interest. Members may be homogeneous, representing one point of view, or heterogeneous, representing many points of view. Group discussions could be formal, using a set list of questions designed to elicit specific information, or informal, with users and potential users chatting about their concerns.

Individuals who have been willing to provide information about needs and concerns of the library are often very helpful in developing strategies to achieve specific goals. People generally are much more willing to participate in a project if they have made contributions to its design. All of the user groups within the school community—teachers, administrators, support staff, and, most important, students—need to have a part in developing the program of library services offered by the media specialist. If people do not find something of value to them in their library, then in actuality it does not exist for them! That is why collaborative efforts are necessary to provide library services that will fulfill their needs. Furthermore, it is almost impossible to offer special events without this type of collaboration.

The school library media specialist has the responsibility of assessing the program of library services as it enfolds, adapting it as needed, and evaluating its success as part of the overall educational infrastructure. If the library is "alive," it will change; that is what will make it a dynamic center for informational and recreational needs. The program of developing library services is a process, and it cannot be stressed enough that this process must have a clear and concrete place within the strategic plan of the school. The media center's program is meant to be a complement to the process, and this flexible plan will enable it to provide the educational resources that are necessary to support the program. Following this process will ensure quality and relevancy in special events.

One of the frustrations that many people have with this process is that it must be reviewed on a regular basis. It is not something that can be done once and then forgotten. One of the best ways for the library to do this on a continual basis is to have a formal marketing plan in place. Most marketing plans used by libraries are designed to target internal audiences (for example, the school community) and external markets through promotions (these will be covered in Chapter 7). An internal marketing plan calls for continuous relationship building with the audiences, not merely occasional interactions. The best marketing strategy is one that states the benefits to the user, and most promotional materials can be designed around this. Writing the plan down provides a framework for reference, and checking it regularly for progress refreshes the spirit. This continued updating is also important because it allows the school media center to keep the staff apprised of national trends, and to adapt and adjust efforts based on current events within the community. This is a challenge, but one that provides us with the opportunity to show our determination to succeed.

The challenge is clearly outlined in *America 2000*, which suggests that "each community must become a place where learning can happen."[6] The school library media center's mission—"to ensure that all staff and students are effective users of information"[7]—meets this challenge by distributing information in a nonjudgmental fashion, and respecting the powerful lessons that can be learned through cultural diversity. Student achievement is at the forefront of this mission.

Our children live in a world where they will continually need to learn and develop new skills throughout their lives. Gone are the days of one job per lifetime. Education must be viewed as a lifelong pursuit. Students must leave the formal education process prepared to continue learning with the skills that they have acquired. In addition to content knowledge, students must be able to investigate and solve problems by evaluating information and drawing conclusions. Because of this, school library media specialists must take their impact on this process more seriously than ever before. We must be accountable for our contributions to this lifelong learning process, and we must be sure that students take with them the ability to use other libraries—academic, public, and special—in their lifelong pursuit of knowledge.

Providing the foundation of skills that can be transferred to other situations is what gives the school library media center its vitality. The commitment that we make is the "secret ingredient" that was identified in *America 2000*. It is the human touch—in the media specialist's case, matching the right information with the right user—and it is our contribution to the perpetuation of civilization.

Putting these concepts into a proactive framework through the use of special events programs makes for a school media center that is alive. This book gives step-by-step advice on how to make special events memorable.

It is intended as a guide; not every step will be applicable to every program. Choose what suits, what is useful, and make it work for you. Then be sure to relax and enjoy your special event.

NOTES

1. *Information Power: Guidelines for School Library Media Programs* (Chicago: American Library Association, 1989), 1.

2. *American Association of School Librarians Position Statement on Flexible Scheduling* (Chicago: American Association of School Librarians, 1991).

3. There are several sources that can assist you in developing your program. Ann Bleakley, *Resource-Based Learning Activities* (American Library Association, 1994): Julie Dorrell, *Resource Based Learning* (McGraw Hill, 1993); Susan Fountain, *Education for Development* (Heinemann, 1995); are good references to check for further information on this topic.

4. *Educational Excellence Through Effective School Media Programs* (Chicago: American Library Association, 1989).

5. *America 2000: An Education Strategy Sourcebook* (Washington, D.C.: U.S. Department of Education, 1991), 12.

6. *America 2000*, 59.

7. *Information Power*, 1.

The Need for Special Events as a Part of the Reading Program

Our multimedia world has conditioned us to expect quality and excitement in presentations. Unless media centers and libraries are able to meet this type of competition head-on, in order to capture the interests of our children, society will be at risk of losing a whole generation of readers. Media centers must take every opportunity to show how much fun reading can be. Special events programs are a tool that school library media specialists can use to their advantage, not only in the ongoing effort to teach children to read, but also to keep that interest alive once they have acquired the skill. We want children to develop reading habits that will stick with them throughout their lives.

In order to offer a special events program in the school library media center, we, as well as the entire school staff, must embrace the idea that these events are essential, not just frills. Programs can be planned for a variety of reasons, but their underlying purpose should be to instill and nurture a love of reading among students. Special events programming gives students a chance to participate actively in learning. Events can be designed to reinforce information presented in the classroom or to pique children's curiosity in new areas. A wide range of activities falls within the category of special events—everything from magic shows, to board games, to contests. I have always worked on the principle that programs should have a literature/reading base. Events can then be a catalyst for children's discovery of books, both fiction and nonfiction, poetry and drama.

Thematic approaches work very well in the school environment, because components of programs can be drawn from the various disciplines. Special programs can stimulate children to practice their writing, strengthen language and vocabulary skills, and encourage them to learn independently. In addition, the thematic approach to programming will more likely keep the various departments of the school working on a collaborative basis, incorporating information from the various disciplines to create a unified learning experience. The value of this is that it exposes the children to content areas in the curriculum in a creative way. Programming encourages communication and cooperation among staff, and it builds the support network which is so critical to the children's enthusiastic participation.

Clearly, there are tremendous cultural benefits for students who have the advantage of special events programs. For example, this may be a musical experience, or exposure to the culture of a foreign country. Although the programming process imposes some additional tasks on the teaching staff, the result is a tremendous aid to the learning process, providing variety, but also allowing repetition of concepts in new ways. Special programs can encourage children to choose reading on their own, and will lead them to other learning experiences through the questions that will inevitably arise. However, the school library media center can only do this work if librarians reach out, understand, and participate in all of the activities, problem solving, and community activities that the school environment provides.

PREPARATION

Preparation is the key to special events programming. Several steps must be taken to set the stage for offering any type of special event. First and foremost, the school library media specialist must prepare a written document that demonstrates the special events program's educational objectives, which are part of the district/state requirements for the academic year. The planning and internal marketing steps discussed in the Introduction must be firmly fulfilled. School library media specialists must be very clear in their own mind about why they are offering the programs. Then they must be able to communicate these reasons to all the other people involved with the school. Expectations and standards for the students must also be clearly expressed at the outset. In the planning stages, different types of learning styles must also be considered. Resource-based learning takes into consideration that all people do not learn in the same way. In order to assist their learning, it is important to provide more than one style of teaching. The adults who are planning the programs must consider how students gather and process information and how they are then able to communicate the information they have absorbed. Thinking about the evaluation process at the outset helps clarify the details needed for the program presentation. It will be of assistance as the teacher evaluates (tests) the learning that has occurred. Giving individual attention to the students through this planning process can build confidence and self-esteem and set the stage for improved academic achievement.

Another essential preliminary step in special events programming is taking stock of the resources already in place within the media center. In some cases, you will be able to budget for additional materials, or find sponsorship for them. However, more often than not, libraries have to make do with what they already have. That is another good reason to focus on content areas in the curriculum, because the needed resources and other materials are usually in place.

Choosing a program that is relevant to the curriculum also helps the school library media center to fulfill the role of nurturing the learning instinct. Planning a multifaceted program gives participants a chance to select the parts that are interesting to them. This maximizes learning and motivates the children as no other technique can. It also reinforces skills that will be useful throughout life, and helps keep up with children's insatiable desire to learn. Programming may serve as an invitation to use the library's other resources, or it may offer educational and cultural experiences that are valuable in themselves.

DETERMINING WHAT KINDS OF PROGRAMS TO OFFER

In developing a schedule of special events, the school library media center must consider the school's priorities and fit programs into that perspective. Using appropriate internal and external marketing strategies will be of great assistance in program planning.

Analyzing what the community needs and wants is a critical part of understanding how to develop programs. It is the responsibility of the school library media specialist to take the time to identify unique aspects of the school community. This process can be accomplished through a variety of techniques. One of the most effective ways is for the media specialist to spend some time simply observing the various school groups in their specific roles. This technique has several advantages, the most significant being that the community does not know that it is being observed. The information gathered is then truly candid. Written opinion surveys are another method. Because they can be filled out anonymously, the information gathered is also honest and natural. One of the disadvantages of this method, however, is that several versions of the survey may be needed to reflect the varying reading levels of the students. Both these methods of data gathering are known as general research.

Specific research, or target marketing, is composed of another set of techniques to gather specific information that is even more useful in determining a programming schedule. As noted in the Introduction, focus groups are one of the most common ways of determining the needs or wants of the community. They can be held with mixed groups consisting of representatives from all the school's populations. They can also be held with homogeneous groups comprising only one segment. An advantage of this research method is that the facilitator of the group can guide the discussion, keeping it focused on the topic at hand. Focus groups can also be structured so that they leave time for social interaction. Refreshments (coffee and pastry or perhaps an afternoon snack) are always welcome!

Another kind of targeted research involves conducting interviews with opinion leaders—for example, school administrators—who can contribute information from individuals outside the school community. Many people influence policy but are not necessarily involved with the school on a day-to-day level. Board of Education representatives, city council/aldermen, parents, and business and community leaders who have a stake in the future of education could be consulted.

To make these methods as productive as possible, it is necessary to motivate or provide incentives for the participants. One of the most successful ways of getting people to respond is letting them know what is in it for them. Although it may sound crass, this method, known as benefit analysis, often meets with success.

General and specific research, in addition to providing the basic information a school library media center needs for planning, has additional benefits. The media center will learn a great deal about how the various groups process information, as well as up-front planning strategies. An additional benefit of these information-gathering techniques is that they are in themselves positive public relations activities. They have the potential of creating or enhancing awareness of the school media center. They also create a positive image of the program. People like being asked about their opinions and ideas. They often begin to feel a sense of ownership in a program if they have been invited to contribute to the process. Work on the premise that school officials need to be convinced that the interruptions in the daily routine are worth it. Getting people involved in the process builds the attitude that these programs *are not* to be missed.

ENCOURAGING LIBRARY USE THROUGH SPECIAL EVENTS PROGRAMS

Using the curriculum as the basis for setting priority levels for programming makes a great deal of sense. However, there are several other reasons why a school library media center might sponsor particular types of programs. Offering incentives or rewards to encourage reading is a common way of bringing children into the media center. The media center also should use this method to encourage the use of different parts of the collection. Programs can be used to introduce poetry, biography, drama, or any area of the collection that the media specialist feels is underutilized.

Programs will make the users look at the school media center in a different way. In addition, programs are often a great boost to the morale of the organization, since they foster teamwork and cooperative efforts. Because they offer something special, they tend to make people feel special themselves. They can help build self-esteem and self-confidence in those who have a hand in planning them. On all levels, programs have the ability to influence behavior and can have a positive impact on the learning experience. Adapting programs in light of the talent, resources, and abilities of current personnel will create the cultural and recreational opportunities that the school needs to offer. Programs designed to reach specific target audiences and achieve particular objectives serve as an invitation to use the available resources. This makes them a valuable experience in themselves.

READING PROGRAMS

Traditionally, reading programs have been the kind most commonly offered by school libraries. It makes sense for a school library media specialist to offer them. The key to developing a *reading habit*, not just the ability to read, is enjoyment. The media center's participation in reading programs for the child's educational development lays the foundation for lifelong literacy. There is general agreement in the profession that reading to children promotes a love of reading and language. Being read to also predisposes children to learn to love reading on their own. Developing the reading habit, along with the corresponding skills of imaginative development, conceptualization, and communication, is the cornerstone of education. This ability will lead to success in the school setting, and then be transferred to life situations.

The importance of reading to the child's cognitive development can not be overemphasized. Reading allows children to change places with the characters and the heroes in the stories. Experience of this sort allows them to develop the confidence that they too can become heroes on their own one day. Nurturing their reading ability can help children reach their potential in all aspects of life. The school library media center can plan follow-up activities to reinforce character development. Mentoring programs can also supplement this reading activity by providing role models for the children to emulate. Parents, grandparents, and community volunteers can work with students on a one-to-one basis to foster reading and provide extra help. Many school systems also have high school students work with elementary school students.

The enhancement of a child's enjoyment of stories through music, props, and puppets gives another dimension to reading and turns the most basic of library services—storytelling—into a special event. The school library can use these additional activities to create memorable experiences for children, ones that they will associate with reading. Many storytellers are purists who cringe at the thought of using these enhancers. The school library media specialist must decide if the long-term value of creating a memorable experience outweighs arguments against using enhancements. Crafts that emphasize an aspect of the stories presented can supplement the reading program quite effectively, or they can be programs in their own right. All of these opportunities set the stage for children not only to enjoy reading, but also to enjoy learning, and to translate that learning into other formats. This positive learning experience can increase the use of the school library media center.

These various activities motivate children, as well as provide informational, cultural, and recreational opportunities. In order to support children as learners, it is important to encourage them to explore and to try new things. Innovative reading programs will make children feel good about experimenting. However, it is equally important to offer situations in which the children can repeat their experiences, because so much learning is done through repetition. Children can become frustrated when trying to learn new skills, so repetition is important. Patience, too, is imperative. The school media specialist must continually strive to encourage children and thus build their confidence in learning.

Reading must be encouraged outside of the school environment as well if the goal of creating a "nation of readers" is ever to be met. School media centers must work in cooperation with public libraries to keep children learning throughout the entire year. Coordinating reading programs is important. Efforts can include joint reading lists, reading clubs/incentive programs, and parent support programs. Implementing this type of program is especially important during school vacations or summer recess. This is another way to encourage children to maintain the skills they have begun to acquire.

Programs are the results of a creative process, and they can and should be evaluated periodically so that they remain fresh and appropriate for the children in the schools. There is no one right way to do programming. School library media centers should consider several possibilities and adapt them to suit their needs, thus providing quality to their patrons.

Book displays are a traditional accompaniment to reading programs. Setting them up a few weeks in advance of the program in a prominent location in the media center is a terrific way to publicize the programs as well as support the program content. These displays will attract the potential participants of a program in a way that a flyer cannot. This may be another way to involve the public library as well. They may be able to loan you extra copies of books, or perhaps put up a display for you. In addition to publicizing upcoming programs, displays graphically illustrate program content and encourage people to use the materials, some of which they may not have known were available.

Promotion becomes even more important when the program is held outside of regular school hours. In some cases it may be necessary for students to find alternate means of transportation to get home if a "late bus" is not available. Many school systems, however, do take after-school programs and activities seriously and provide the needed transportation. Alternatively, parents may need to be available to pick up their children after the program ends. Putting this all together requires a great deal of hard work by the school library media specialist and the support staff. However, the satisfaction that is gained when children love to read is well worth the effort.

On Your Mark, Get Set, Program! Developing Special Events Programs Relevant to the Curriculum

2

ON YOUR MARK

If you have followed the process outlined in Chapter 1, chances are that the concept of special events programming has come to be accepted by your school's faculty and staff. You should now be positioned to develop specific programs complete with learning objectives. Truly, you are now "on your mark," and have momentum behind you to freely articulate specific, clear, and simple aims for the program. Be certain that the ideas are appropriate for your particular school and that they are relevant in content. You will also need to be able to demonstrate measurable learning outcomes in students.

GET SET: FINDING RESOURCES FOR SPECIAL EVENTS PROGRAMS

What makes a good special events program? Where do the ideas come from? Inspiration for special events is everywhere! You must keep an open mind and be receptive to ideas, even when you may not consciously be looking for them. An advertisement on television, a current event, a cartoon in a magazine, or a vacation experience may spur a program idea. Sometimes ideas come when you least expect them, and the timing is just not right to hold a special event. For this reason, I strongly recommend developing a resource file. There is no one right way to do this; the important principle is to find a method that will help develop the idea for you. Use your resource file to organize and store ideas for future use, so that you will be able to find something quickly when you need it.

Some programmers prefer note cards in a file box; others use notebooks. In some cases you may have much information, in others only a word of two. Figures 2.1 and 2.2 show sample ideas that need much more thought to become programs. However, they may generate a list of activities when the time is right.

Figure 2.1
Sample Program Idea

Subject:	Families/Tradition
Idea:	Ethnic brunch/dinner
Curricula Applications:	Social Studies units—Diversity—Grade 8
Source:	Article in women's magazine on how one family tried to preserve traditions
Possible Activities:	Ethnic foods in café "Pot Luck" evening or Saturday morning Oral histories or family stories Projects with elementary schools
Media Center Resources:	Literature: *Stone Soup* For Elementary: *How My Parents Learned to Eat* Folktales
Community Resources:	Community or ethnic centers; churches
Other:	Sell tickets and ask community to attend

Figure 2.2
Sample Program Idea

Subject:	Seasonal Grade Level—Varied
Idea:	Scarecrow Contest
Source:	Driving through Sturbridge today, I saw a scarecrow contest on a local green, with entries from families as well as individuals. Would be great to do with classes entering one each?
Curricula Applications:	Agriculture/Why do we have scarecrows? Natural Materials/Recycling Folklore
Media Center Resources:	*Wizard of Oz* among others!

On Your Mark, Get Set, Program! 19

Another idea is to keep a list of potential resource people as you find them, because, again, you never know when you may need them (Figure 2.3 gives an example). Names can be arranged alphabetically or by subject. You may want to experiment to see what system works best for you.

Figure 2.1 shows an idea in the process of becoming a program. The school media specialist can then proceed to make logistical arrangements to carry out the programs, and begin to make contacts to see what parts of the idea can be developed. Related ideas may develop as other people learn of your project. Perhaps someone knows a good dance group or music group; a performance could coincide with the brunch/dinner. Perhaps the middle school students can share experiences that they have had in school with younger grades. Or they can share literature, with older students reading to younger students.

Likewise, the idea in Figure 2.2 is not completely developed, but the thread is there. Later, we will see some of the logistics that had to be arranged before this idea developed into a successful program.

Figure 2.3 shows a resource file card. Again, the basics are there as a reminder when you want to follow up on an idea. Other notes that could be added include discussions you may have had with the person; if a fee is charged and, if so, how much; or any special requirements.

The possibilities for finding ideas and resource people through this casual observation method truly are endless. When the ideas are mixed with a little creativity, some wonderful special events can result. However, this method is done primarily on an individual basis, and other methods need to be employed as well. Brainstorming sessions are recommended as a way to bring in new perspectives, and, indeed, to test out some ideas before too much planning is done. Brainstorming sessions, like focus groups, can be formalized, but participants are much more likely to express candid thoughts and ideas if the sessions are formal. Talking over coffee in the teachers' lounge or in the cafeteria generates ideas to which people become attached, and which they are likely to support. Be prepared, however, to have your original ideas greatly change, or even be

Figure 2.3
Sample Resource Listing

Subject: Music

Jane Riell
91 Quarry Road
Tel. number:

Plays Piano, Guitar

---

totally revamped in this process. In the long run, this is great, because people are motivated by the ideas they create and you have a true "test" to see if you have support. It is better to leave behind an idea that no one likes but you than to develop it and have no one attend the event!

Networking outside of the school community is another way of finding resources. Various groups and organizations may have programs that can be useful to your school. There are many ways of sharing expenses for programs if they are offered on the same day or on consecutive days within a limited geographic radius. Block bookings are beneficial to the performers as well as to the school media center, so do not hesitate to suggest this as a possibility.

Organizations that might not immediately come to mind should also be considered. For example, symphony orchestras are often very eager to cooperate with the schools. Live performance can add a new perspective to the curriculum on music theory, as students experience music firsthand rather than through recordings. Interdisciplinary learning activities could also be incorporated. Activities could focus on the customs, costumes, and traditions of the era in which the music was written. And the life of the composer could be introduced as a way of exposing children to biography as a genre. This type of programming is beneficial to the symphony as well. Playing some selections from an upcoming concert may encourage students and their families to attend full performances, perhaps awakening the interest of students who might become subscribers for a lifetime. It is also appropriate to request some free tickets so that a drawing for them can be held at the end of the program.

There are also some formal ways of identifying program resources. Numerous directories are published that are very useful for this purpose. For example, local and state arts councils may publish directories of artists within a city or state. Musicians, artists, and actors often belong to unions and professional associations which may have state chapters as well as national affiliations. These are important contacts for two reasons. Not only will the sources be able to provide complete and current information about individuals, including addresses, phone numbers, agents, and so on, but very often these groups also subsidize performances to make them more affordable. Colleges, universities, hospitals, and many corporations publish speakers' bureau lists. The organization of these lists varies, but there is usually some sort of subject listing, which is very convenient if you are looking for a specific program to meet a need in a given area of the curriculum. Talks are often offered as a public service, and often the individuals listed can be engaged for a modest fee, or at no charge. This makes them especially attractive for those with low budgets.

The marketing departments of major publishers are another important resource that can be very helpful in planning special events programs. Many of their authors tour the country to promote their new works, and are often willing to talk to school groups. Children especially like to hear about how authors get their ideas, and how they learned to write books.

Professional booking agents are another way of identifying and booking resources. They are listed in the yellow pages of most city telephone directories. This may indeed be the only way to book some people, especially those of celebrity status. However, be cautious when using booking agents as resources. Their job is to find placement for their clients, for a fee. That fee also includes their remuneration as middleman, which is totally appropriate but may drive the cost over your budget.

THE YEARLY PLANNING CALENDAR

Another useful recommendation is to develop a yearly planning calendar. This will allow you to look at the activities that you want to offer in the school library media center as a whole and compare them with the overall calendar of the school. Coordinating special events programs with major curriculum subjects is helpful for several reasons. First and foremost is timing. You do not want to put a tremendous amount of effort into an event and find out later that it conflicts with other activities that would likely attract the same audience. Second, it helps in the overall planning of the event to leave enough lead time for advertising, plan development, logistical arrangements, and so on. Third, a yearly calendar provides an overview of the quality of the educational programs that are coordinated with the learning that is taking place within the school. It also assists you in scheduling and in assigning the necessary tasks involved in organizing special events. This really puts to good use the philosophy that the school faculty has a responsibility to trigger students' learning by making use of natural curiosity, imagination, and creativity. The students as well as the faculty can and should be involved in developing the calendar, and thus programming planning.

A yearly planning calendar of this sort makes a good promotional tool in itself. You should add a little clip art, copy it on some attractive color stock, and distribute it widely throughout the school, school system, or community.

In a school or college setting, it makes good sense to organize the calendar on the academic year (see Figures 2.4 and 2.5). While the outline is simple, it indicates the value of the process.

First of all, let us examine some of the key elements of this scheduling outline. There are very definite times of highly programmed activities—most notably October and April—and times when the schedule is a bit lighter, as in March. There are two main reasons for this "peak and valley" approach to the schedule. First, activities are done in coordination with other main items in the school's schedule. It is especially important to avoid conflicts with examinations or other mandated activities. Second, this approach

Figure 2.4
Sample Elementary School Media Center Program Calendar

September

"Library After Hours"
3–5 P.M.
Tuesday and Thursday
Stay after school, have a snack,
and see what the library has for you!
Display: "Homework Helpers"

October

"Parents' Night Inn," Oct. 25, 6–9 P.M.
All parents who visit during parents' night are
eligible to win a weekend at a country inn.
October 25–31
"Scarecrow Exhibits and Class Competition"

November

"Families Reading Together"
Book Week   Book Fair

December

"Celebrating Our Diversity"
A month-long medley of programs highlighting
the cultures of the world's peoples.

January/February

"Finding Our Past—Celebrating Our Future"
Family histories, ethnic food brunch, and technology exhibit

March

"So It Is Spring!"
Book display about spring plants, animals, etc.

April

School Library Media Month
Emphasis on the various programs of the school media center
All month "Write to Read" program
featuring guest author visits

May/June

"Till We Meet Again"
Nurturing the reading habit during the summer

Figure 2.5
Sample High School Media Center Program Calendar

September
"Library After Hours"
3–5 P.M.
Monday and Wednesday
After school learn about new
information sources that will help you in your courses!
Refreshments served.
Display: "We've Got the Answer"

October
"Parents' Night Inn," Oct. 25, 6–9 P.M.
Parents are invited to check out the school media resources and the
guidance office for materials on college selection and financial aid.
All parents who visit during this parents' night can
register to win a weekend at a country inn.

November
"Internet: Our International Online Information Tool"

December
"Across Our Cultures"
A celebration of traditions through literature,
in coordination with the language department
Dec. 10–15, 2–5 P.M.

January/February
"A Celebration of Ethnic Poetry"
Featuring black, Latino, and Native American works

March
CD-ROM Fair
Tuesday and Thursday, 12 noon–3 P.M.
Try our new databases.

April
School Library Media Month
Guest authors featured

May/June
Tuesdays at "Good Summer Reads,"
School Media Specialist Joseph and English faculty Fay, Donner, and
Eliot will provide you with some sizzling summer reading ideas.

---

gives the media center staff adequate time to prepare for the big special events without impairing their ability to provide quality library services on a daily basis.

Another important feature of the schedule is that it builds on other activities that the school has already planned. For example, "Parents' Night Inn" is based on Parents' Night, and the book fair, which encourages students to purchase their own books, is scheduled to coincide with parent visits to the school for conferences. Seasonal activities can be incorporated into the schedule to build on the mounting excitement that people already are experiencing, while adding a learning dimension. Celebrating diversity during holiday seasons is a way to introduce new cultures and the many aspects that comprise them: language, folklore, customs, dress, traditions. Certainly there are numerous ways to tie such a program into the curriculum units. The program might encourage different activities for social life, as well as for mathematics and language lessons.

To clarify this process, it is helpful to look at some of the specifics involved with the programs illustrated in Figure 2.4. "Library After Hours" requires a commitment on the part of the media center staff to stay at work after the media center normally closes. This program recognizes that not all students are able to use the media center as much as they would like during the normal school day; that there are children at home after school with no adult supervision; that children may not be able to get to the public library; and that students are hungry after a long school day and need a snack to hold them until dinner. The media center staff does not do any technical work during this period (ordering materials, processing them, etc.). Rather, 100 percent of their attention is focused on the students in the media center on that day. This program makes time available for students to learn how to research a topic from the basics, to study a topic in depth, to use a computer (which they may not have at home), or simply to talk to the media specialist about books, or about themselves.

"Parents' Night Inn" is planned to take place during conference periods. It gives the media specialist the opportunity to show parents what is in the media center, to explain upcoming projects to them, to request assistance with special projects, to demonstrate databases, and so on. A drawing for a stay at a country inn may entice parents to attend the program; the prize may be donated by an inn or hotel. The media specialist's attitude and approach to the parents will be what makes them return! "Scarecrow Exhibits and Class Competition" is a way of bringing the media center into the main loop of activity by generating some school and class spirit. For this program, the media specialist sets the criteria for a scarecrow decorating competition among classes. Interesting criteria can tie into lessons that are being taught that month, or may even be tied to famous book characters. Appropriate prizes could include a pizza party or another school-sanctioned healthy treat, sets of bookmarks, pens, pencils, folders for the students in the class, or a collection of books that remains in the winning classroom.

"Families Reading Together" is another opportunity to encourage parent participation in their children's education, a strong underlying principle of *America 2000*. The school media specialist can set up displays of materials that are good read-alouds, encourage extended families (grandparents, aunts, uncles, neighbors) to read aloud with the children, and generally promote reading as a habit. Traditionally, Children's Book Week falls in November, and many libraries and media centers sponsor book fairs at which books are sold. It makes good sense to integrate activities of this type into your program, since children will be accompanied by an adult who could buy materials. A word of caution: Be sure to have some opportunity for those who cannot afford to buy materials to get them another way. Perhaps the PTA or parents' association can provide funding so that a number of books can be given away. This might also be arranged with the company that is doing the book fair. Refreshments at activities of this kind are also important. They should be simple and easy to serve, but they add an air of friendliness to the overall atmosphere of the program. This translates into the media center saying "welcome" loud and clear!

"Celebrating Our Diversity" is a way of using the resources of the school district and the school population in an effort to better understand one another. This is an opportunity to showcase the dance, music, crafts, traditions, games, foods, language, and literature of diverse cultures and ethnic groups. Programs on cultural diversity can be planned as a series, stressing different activities on certain days (for example, dance on Monday, foods on Wednesday) and encompassing several cultures, or a week can be assigned to each culture.

"Finding Our Past" is an example of a program that can segue directly into other topics. By January or February in the academic year, the students are comfortable with the environment of the school library media center. They can use their acquired skills to learn more about their ancestors. They might want to learn about the area where they are living from a genealogical as well as a historical perspective. New resources such as computer programs to build family trees are appropriate tools. The students then can develop some vision of where they will be in the future. This type of program would need to be designed with various levels of difficulty, depending on the age of the participants. Young children might enjoy a treasure hunt approach, while high school students/young adults might be more motivated by reading the diaries of their ancestors. It is always an eye opener for children to learn that their parents and grandparents were once their age! The media specialist might have access to diaries through the local historical society. Students could read them and then use a similar format to write their own diaries. Students will need to use critical thinking skills to make some educated guesses about years in the future. How will their grandchildren find out about them (e.g., will the information be on a diskette, not in a diary?)? "What will their jobs be?" "What tools will they need to do them?" are just two of the many questions they might want to pursue in the media center.

Making a time capsule is an enjoyable experience for students of all ages. This is an appropriate special activity that fits well into the project. It is also inexpensive. If done properly, it can involve many different people from the community. Time capsules also make terrific human interest stories for the local press.

As noted earlier, it is good to have some peak periods on your calendar, and some with fewer activities. March is a good time to plan and prepare for School Library Media Month, celebrated in April. Because of the intensity of that planning, it may be advisable to schedule a program in March that is not too time-consuming. "So It Is Spring!" is a way to bring to light materials that are seasonally appropriate, for example books on plants, animals, and gardening. There certainly are programs that can go along with them if time permits. A demonstration program on how to start seedlings is an example. However, for the busy school library media specialist, a book display may be quite enough.

A plan for programming allows one to pace oneself and to focus on the large programs that need the most attention. School Library Media Month is such an example. It was developed nationally to give the media specialist an opportunity to promote and to focus attention on the school media center, so every effort should be made to make this an effective program. Efforts to create an awareness of the local program are usually reinforced by state and national efforts at this time as well.

In the sample calendar, the "Write to Read" program is featured during this time. It is intended to provide a bit of a twist to the traditional reading program. The emphasis is on helping students develop writing skills and the ability to communicate ideas. This flexible program can take on many facets that can be adapted to various grade levels. Some possibilities are author visits, in which the author shares his/her experiences in writing books; write-your-own-book programs, through which students write, illustrate, and have their book displayed in the media center; or a resource-based learning project which provides the framework for some interdisciplinary instructional units that allow integration of information and technology skills with the content area objectives.

Finally, "Till We Meet Again" is a way of supplying students with appropriate summer reading lists, activities, and so on. The program should be done in cooperation with the teachers and tied into the subject areas that the students will cover in the new school year. This program could include a visit from the public librarian, who can tell students about events that will be sponsored by the library over the summer.

All of these suggestions lend themselves to press opportunities. Photos of the programs, perhaps a feature interview with the guest author, or publication of the students' work in the newspaper will provide an opportunity for those in the community to share in these activities. For people who do not have children in the school system, this is an especially important area of concern. Far too often, news about youth is not positive; you have provided a snapshot of the positive. Those of us who work with young people know kids are great, but it may be easy to overlook that fact when you don't have day-to-day contact with them. This type of publicity has far-reaching capabilities. If you made a good impression, you have created new allies. These allies (taxpayers) are important to you at budget time.

As noted above, many state and national efforts are in place to assist media specialists in planning and promoting school library media month. It is important to contact your state library association and to network with local colleagues. Possible benefits include tapping into a network of ideas; taking advantage of block booking discounts with programs; finding a source for mass-produced flyers, posters, handouts, and bookmarks; sharing the expense of advertising; and using the principle of strength in numbers to attract media attention.

National association information is also important. You may be able to tie your program in with a particular theme; take advantage of promotional campaigns that are in place; purchase commercially prepared graphic materials; and use the fact that it is School Library Media Month nationally to invite local and state government officials to issue proclamations for local use. Chapter 9 provides information on contacting these groups.

After a month of extensive programming, I recommend a lower profile for the next month. As the end of the academic year approaches, bear in mind other school activities, such as field trips, examinations, and year-end wrapup for the faculty. It will also give you time to evaluate the programs presented and to put together recommendations for programs to be held again. However, it is important to plan some sort of activity that not only ties your programs together but also encourages children to read during the vacation period. Distribution of reading lists, visits from the public librarian, and perhaps even an assembly to congratulate the students on their participation will serve as motivators in the learning process. Academic awards ceremonies should have as many dignitaries as you can arrange, from both the school and the community. This makes the event special for the students, and it is another way to humanize your publicity.

This calendar gives you an idea of how effective planning can create a year-long coordinated school library media center plan. It works because programs are put down in advance, and you are not scrambling at the last minute to build support for them or to find adequate space to hold them because someone else beat you to it. The calendar also works because it forces the planner to make conscious decisions about the offerings and to make sure that they fit into the curriculum in a timely fashion. Developing a calendar outline will also save you time in the long run. Remember, too, that it is never cast in stone, and it can and should be changed and adapted if circumstances warrant.

GETTING STARTED: TURNING IDEAS INTO PROGRAMS

Once you have established a general plan, you are ready to begin actual preparations for the programs. The following pages present examples of forms and worksheets that will actually walk you through the planning process. While at the outset they might seem fussy and time-consuming, over time their value will become apparent. They are time savers and they help assure that you have paid enough attention to the details that special events programming requires. These forms are designed as guidelines. In order for them to be most effective, you will need to adapt them to suit your particular library. File them and keep them for future use with an evaluation sheet when the program is complete. This file will help you correct things that didn't work quite the way you wanted, and serve as a reminder of which programs you will want to repeat and which were unsuccessful. In any case, it will provide you with a short-cut method for future planning.

Figure 2.6 shows a program overview worksheet, a tool to help think through a program idea. The form notes the staff member who is in charge of the program, and the date. It encourages the use of a title from the beginning, an important consideration because it will help the program take on an identity. This is further developed in the program description, a one or two sentence summary of what the program is expected to be, and in the program objective, which states the purpose of the program and what it is expected to accomplish. The planner needs to keep in mind those who will benefit (target audience and needs assessment). This is important information for outside presenters, who will need to target their presentations to be appropriate for a particular age group and to fill a specific need. The worksheet also serves as a reminder that the program should be designed to fit into the learning profile of the school (goals, coordination).

This worksheet is an important first step in planning, as it forces you to think about what staff is required and what skills they need in order to make the program successful. In addition, it reminds the planner that it is perfectly acceptable to go beyond the school library media center staff to find other personnel to meet particular program requirements. The beginnings of the budget process are in this form as well. As you begin to think about outside resources, speakers, materials, and so on, you begin to project how much money will be needed to make the program successful. Finally, estimating a timetable begins to put the program into the daily

Figure 2.6
Program Overview Worksheet

Staff Planner _____ Proposed Date _____
Program Title

1. Target Audience:
2. Program Description:
3. Program Objective:
4. Length and Frequency:
5. Relationship to Media Center Goals:
6. Relationship to School/District Goals:
7. Needs Assessment:
8. Evaluation Process:
9. Coordination with Other School Events:
10. Staffing Requirements:
11. Other Staffing:
12. Resources Required:
    Materials:
    Speakers:
    Estimated Cost:
13. Estimated Timetable for Implementation:
    Dates: Activities:
14. Other:

schedule, as the need to meet specific deadlines approaches. Gathering and recording this information is very useful preparation, giving you the facts you will need to answer the inevitable questions that will arise.

Your idea now is well on its way to becoming a program. The next step is to determine how much space will be needed and what kind of space is appropriate for this type of program. Plan with the everyday schedule in mind so that there will be no interruptions in the delivery of basic library services, and so that you will not unnecessarily disrupt other activities that are happening in the school. Figure 2.7 shows a sample worksheet for planning logistical details.

Figure 2.7
Event Logistics Worksheet

Program Name _____

Program Date _____ Time _____

Program Location _____

Room Setup:
    ☐ = Tables   TT = Podium
    XXX = Chairs   ☒ = Stage

No. of Chairs ____

No. of Tables ____

AV Equipment Needed:

Other Equipment Needed:

Refreshments:

Other:

Figure 2.8
Risk Assessment Questionnaire

[ ] [ ] RISK CODE
Name of Activity/Event _____
Location of Activity_____
Start-up Date _____ Completion Date _____
Participating Parties _____
_____
_____

Brief Description _____
_____
_____
_____
_____

Safety Controls _____
_____
_____

Responsible Department/Division _____
Contact Person/Telephone _____

                              Prepared by
                              _____
                              Signature

                              _____
                              Department/Division

Key to Risk Codes
01   Contracts, leases, agreements
02   Assemblies, parades, celebrations
03   Construction
04   Operations, services, processes, programs
05   Equipment, materials
06   Special activities
07   Other

If you are not holding the special event in the media center, you may need to reserve space in some other area of the school. Procedures on this will vary. Some schools will have forms to complete. Others may keep a booking calendar that reserves space. Still others may require official approval. It is important to learn the procedures of your facility, and confirm your booking needs with the proper authority. It would be very discouraging to go through the process of planning a special event and then find no space available for the program. This form will provide you with a confirmation of your reservation (you should file it with whoever is in charge of the physical plant of the school), and it serves as a checklist to remind you to take care of all the logistical details. This is especially important if the event is not going to be held in your domain—the school library media center—but in another location in the school, for example, the auditorium, the cafeteria, or the gymnasium.

Some municipalities may require you to file risk statements or liability waivers for all programming (see Figure 2.8). If this is the case, add this to your event logistics worksheet as well and complete all the necessary paperwork involved.

In completing these forms you are compiling, step by step, a record that will prove useful not only in preparing this event, but in the future if repeat performances are anticipated. By compiling brief, accurate records, you are developing a very efficient programming system. This is one secret to repeating successes but not mistakes.

If you have made it this far in the program plan, you have succeeded in overcoming the hardest part of the process—getting started. Your program overview gives you a jump start in planning, but does not lock you into a hard and fast schedule. Its flexibility is one of its greatest assets. Using the overview in coordination with more detailed forms will put you well on the way to programming success. If you are careful to coordinate events with the curriculum, and keep them relevant, you will find teachers and students eager to participate.

PROGRAM FORMAT

The next step, determining the basic format for the program, should be done simultaneously with the logistical arrangements. The format depends on the content of the program and your program goals. This will then lead to the next major decision: Who will do the program? There are many programs that school library media specialists can offer on their own. However, the term "special events" means that you are bringing in people other than yourself to present the program. Possibilities include speakers, performers of various kinds, authors, entertainers, and so on.

Effective programmers must consider the overall impact of the choices they make. The budget available for programming is one of the major factors in determining whether the program will be done by the staff in-house or by an invited guest. Budget information is provided later in this chapter as it relates to some of the program considerations. Chapter 8 focuses on ways to locate funds and make the best use of the financial resources available.

ORGANIZING THE PROGRAM

What skills are needed to be an effective programmer? Generally speaking, events programmers need to be detail-oriented and organized, flexible enough to accommodate changes, committed to hard work, and able to sustain a high energy level. Coupling these characteristics with the planning process will help bring these programs to fruition. One of the tools that is very helpful to the programmer planner is an event scheduler (see Figure 2.9).

Figure 2.9
Event Scheduler

5–12 mos. prior to event	Recruit and meet with a committee Decide purpose of the event Target the audience Brainstorm ideas/themes Select/confirm site; use event scheduler checklist Name event/name date
3–5 mos. prior to event	Hold regular committee meetings Develop a budget Look for a sponsor Outline the program Contact performers/speakers Sign contracts Send out publicity to newsletters Develop flyers
1–2 mos. prior to event	Concentrate on program details Send out more publicity Continue to meet with committee Put up book displays
2 weeks prior to event	Hold press conference/interviews
1 week prior to event	Make name tags, signs, and other items Reconfirm speaker Print programs Check all arrangements
Event Day	Put up directional signs Begin event officially Introduce speaker Welcome participants Conclude and clean up
1 day to 2 weeks after event	Write thank-yous Complete budget report Evaluate program

Using a scheduler like this provides the programmer with a useful checklist so that given tasks are accomplished within a particular time frame. Furthermore, it provides an ongoing evaluation method, so changes that would improve the program outcome can be implemented.

The scheduler also helps break down the various tasks so that some of them may be delegated to other individuals in the school community. This helps not only to spread the work around (in many cases particular functions can be assigned to a resident expert), but also to build an understanding of the whys and wherefores of the special event.

There are times when it would be helpful to have a committee to work with on a special event. There are some good reasons for managing the event this way. You will find that when more people are involved, they bring different perspectives and abilities to planning the project as well as sharing the workload that goes along with the preparation. Group participation also helps to promote the special program, because committee members will be in touch with each other and their friends about what they are doing. All committees need direction and leadership. This role will fall to you as the media specialist.

Figure 2.10
Special Event Committee Structure

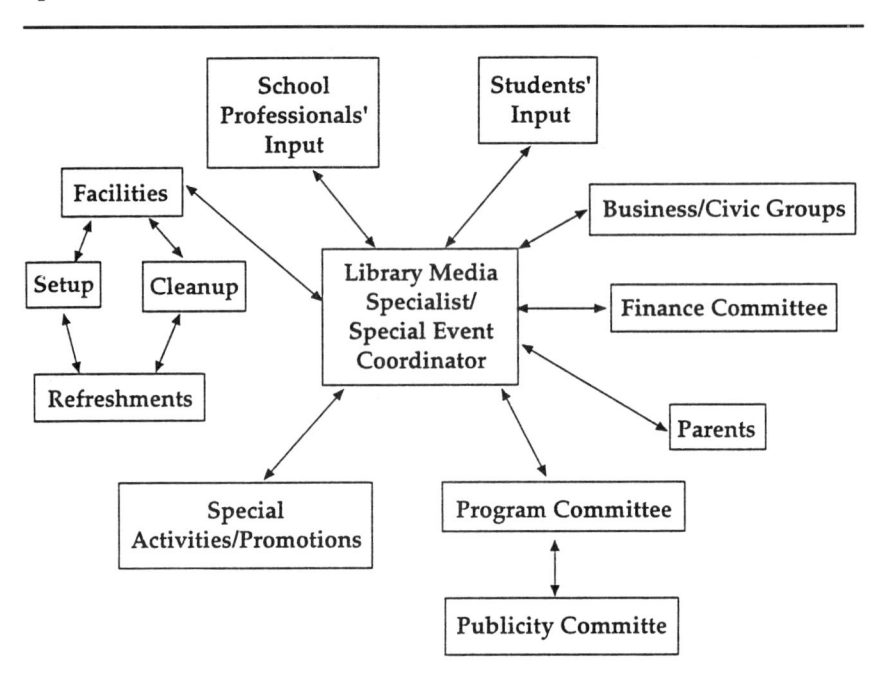

The level of intensive committee work is often determined by the scope of the special event and the ongoing organization within the school. Figure 2.10 is designed to be inclusive and to cover a wide range of possible activities. By no means should the event planner feel that the committee must be in place to begin with. These are simply suggestions and, again, flexibility and adaptation are key elements. Many tasks can be covered by the same person. Additionally, not every program will involve all these components; Figure 2.10 provides an example of possibilities to help you guide the project.

MODEL PROGRAMS THAT WORK

Taking these procedures and processes under consideration, we are now ready to look a little more closely at a particular project model. Working through the forms will give you a good idea of how to plan these activities.

Model Program: The Author Connection

Although school libraries do not often generate vast amounts of book sales, authors and illustrators of children's books are often very eager to visit the schools and to talk with their main audience—young people. Young people are very responsive to authors. Children love to meet their favorites and to hear about how they started writing or where they get their ideas. Giving students the opportunity to interact with creative minds is an experience that is best provided through this type of program. As stated earlier, one of the major objectives of programming is to promote reading as an enjoyable rather than a tedious experience. Giving children a chance to meet writers is one of the most significant ways of accomplishing this. Planning is important when putting on such a program.

As you begin to fill out the worksheets and schedules described earlier, you can see the program beginning to take on a life of its own. (For example, Figure 2.11 shows a completed example of Figure 2.6.) When you complete the forms, you also are providing an ongoing record of your program's progress. This is especially useful for future programs and helps you evaluate the program at its completion.

Do not feel that you have to do it all yourself. When planning a program of this scope, do not be afraid to ask for help. Most of the major publishers employ publicists and marketing personnel who can be of tremendous help in planning your program. Their job is to promote the authors and their books, so they will be very accommodating. A major key to success is to start early, because the publishers have so many requests for their authors. Your request might originally be made on the

Figure 2.11
Program Overview

Staff Planner: M. Trotta

Proposed Date: 4/20/95

Program Title: Meet the Author

1. Target Audience:	Grades 4, 5, 6
2. Program Description:	Author/Illustrator Anne E. Jones will visit and talk about getting started in writing.
3. Program Objective:	The students will have an opportunity to hear from one of their favorite authors and be motivated to read and write on their own.
4. Length and Frequency:	The program will be held on one day, during School Library Media Month.
5. Relationship to Media Center Goals:	The students will be motivated to read more and use the resources of the media center.
6. Relationship to School/District Goals:	Program will help children reach the goal of being able to evaluate their reading and develop critical thinking skills.
7. Needs Assessment:	During informational sessions with the faculty, the faculty indicated that having a famous guest would be a way of motivating students. It is hoped that students would want to be "like the author" and would work to achieve this.
8. Evaluation Process:	Student reading will be tracked before and after event to see if it increases. Students' work will be entered into the library media center as books to evaluate writing process.
9. Coordination with Other School Events:	This will be held during School Library Media Month. It will be coordinated with parents' club book sale so that students will be able to buy copies of the author's books for autographing.
10. Staffing Requirements:	School media specialist, clerk, reading teacher, classroom teachers for all sections of each grade.
11. Other Staffing:	Parent volunteers for book sale and cafeteria staff for "Lunch with the Author" segment. Author's publicist/agent.
12. Resources Required:	Materials: Copies of all author's books Speaker: (Author)

Figure 2.11 (continued)

13. Estimated Timetable for Implementation:	*About 10 months*	
	Sept.	Needs assessment
	Oct.	Contact publisher
	Nov.	Confirm author
	Dec.	Work with parent committee on book sale
		Work with teachers on preparing students on author
	Jan.	Write article for school newsletter
	Feb.	Develop menu for author lunch
	Mar.	Put up book display
		Send press kit to local media
		Call news media contacts
	Apr.	Hold book sale
		Hold event
	May	Write thank-yous
		Enter student writings into library
14. Other:	Invite media specialists from other schools in town and neighboring towns.	

---

phone, but it is a very good idea to put it in writing with as much detail as possible. You will need to be able to describe the accommodations, the number of presentations needed, what the audience will be like, and so on. It is also a good idea to request more than one of the publisher's authors. Since most have busy writing schedules, it is often difficult for them to get away; giving their publicists some choices to work with will increase your chances of getting one of the authors you request. Again, thinking the process through with a form helps. (Figure 2.12 shows a completed example of Figure 2.7.)

As you work with the publisher, you will need to keep in mind the obligations for which the school library media center will be responsible. These might include travel expenses, hotel accommodations and meals, and an honorarium for the author. These items form the beginnings of your budget plans (see Figure 2.13).

In Figure 2.13 you will see that there is a calculation for both staff and volunteer time. While these are, in actuality, in-kind donations, it is critical to outside funders that you provide them with this information. In my experience, funders are not inclined to pay for ongoing operational expenses, such as utilities or salaries. However, they are interested in knowing that these are being assumed by the organization that is asking for their support. It is a different approach with which most of us are

Figure 2.12
Event Logistics Plan

Program Name:	Meet the Author
Program Date:	4/20/95 Time: 1 P.M.
Program Location:	Auditorium
Room Setup:	Table for book signing All lights on Two tables in back for book sale
AV Equipment:	Microphone
Refreshments:	Lunch in cafeteria Make arrangements for parent volunteers to eat lunch in cafeteria
Other:	Have pitcher of water and glass for author
Programmer:	M. Trotta

unfamiliar. If we are going to work closely with the corporate sector and with foundations, then we must consider their methods.

The cost per student for this program is actually $13, and the entire program is just $1000 to $1200 more than was actually being spent by the school system to provide media services anyway. Figure 2.14 illustrates the point by showing you how you might plan to meet the expenses for a special events program. There is the in-kind donation that the school system would make at the outset for staffing. This does more than provide basic support. It also proves the school's commitment to the project, which is a critical factor in convincing other funders to contribute.

Additions could be made to the program that would add more flexibility, making it suitable for all children in the school. Adding other activities by age is one way to extend it. For example, the fourth grade could imagine that they are changing places with the heroes and the characters in the guest author's stories. This process can help the children believe that they, too, may become heroes one day. This possibility can be shared by all children if time is spent nurturing their reading. A follow-up program to reinforce this hero modeling might be a mentoring program using adult personnel in the school. An additional step for sixth graders could be to bring in community leaders from all types of professions in order to teach children success-oriented strategies. Through modeling behavior techniques such as this one, children are able to learn goal-setting and decision-

Figure 2.13
Special Events Budget: Expenses

Site:
    Room $ 0

    Staffing:
        Media Specialist   Clerk
        3 hrs × 20 wks = 60 hrs   5 hrs × 20 wks = 100 hrs
        60 hrs × $20 = $1,200   100 hrs × $9 = $900
                                                             $2,100
    Equipment   0
                                            Subtotal $2,100

Refreshments:
    300 children × $2 $ 600
    Food: 6 volunteers × $3   18
    Beverage: 1 urn coffee   3
    Staffing: 4 hrs × 2 staff
        8 hrs × $10   80
                                      Subtotal $ 701

Programming:
    Performer (author) $ 500
    Travel, hotel   400
    Meals   50
                                      Subtotal $ 950

Decorations: Subtotal $ 20 $ 20

Prizes: Subtotal $ 20 $ 20

Publicity:
    Printing/photocopying $ 50
    Postage   10
    Other   0
                                      Subtotal $ 60

Miscellaneous:
    Telephone/fax $ 30
    Stationery   5
    Other   30
                                      Subtotal $ 65

                                      Total Needed $3,916

Figure 2.14
Special Events Budget: Income

Budget—line item	$ 300
In-kind support	1,800
Donations:	
Corporate	500
Organizations	400
Other	0
Sales:	
Book sales	300
Other support:	600
(Student lunches)	
Total Income	$3,900

making skills. Younger students, for example, second graders, could do an art/craft project about something in the books.

If all of these components are followed faithfully, a successful author-visit program will be the result. You will offer a quality program that meets the needs of your school; at the same time, the media center will gain recognition as a vital force in the educational process.

OTHER PROGRAM IDEAS

This basic procedure can be applied to numerous other ideas to develop them into successful special events. Many programs will have budgets that are much smaller. Possibilities include book talk or book club programs led by the school library media specialist, aimed at introducing students to particular books. Having a student book club, where students review new books, is another wonderful program. The students' opinions are held in high regard by their peers, and a recommendation of this sort might be just the encouragement a student needs to read. This works well with both middle school and high school students.

Reading clubs are an appropriate way to encourage youth to develop reading skills and to introduce them to library materials that they might not select on their own. They also see, through these opportunities, that reading is an enjoyable leisure activity. Discussion sessions also allow them to develop personal relationships.

Theme approaches to special events tend to create lasting impressions in the minds of students, and these often work very well with the established school curriculum. The themes can be about anything, including seasonal celebrations, but they most definitely should be interdisciplinary. Some examples include "Medieval Studies"—the social studies curriculum might cover the historical information; the fine arts department might contribute a study of the artwork and architecture; the music department might cover the music of the time, and coordinate with the language arts department on ballads; the physical education department might sponsor jousting contests, complete with class color banners; and the cafeteria might provide a medieval lunch. Students could be encouraged to research costumes (actual period clothing) in the media center, and they might be introduced to some of the great literature that reflects the times. Depending on the age level, T. H. White's *Once and Future King* or Marguerite di Angeli's *Door in the Wall*, among numerous others, would tie the program together. A festival of this type has many possibilities for involving the community as well.

Other themes that have been successful include "Ancient Games," with activities focused on ancient historical events, and "Reading Around the World," focusing on the world's cultures, languages, peoples, customs, and traditions. "I Have a Dream," using Martin Luther King, Jr.'s speech as the kickoff, can tie in other figures from black history as well as the rich literary heritage of the black community.

Storytelling, while a traditional staple of library and media center programs, provides a tremendous opportunity for special events. The storyteller may be the school library media specialist or another member of the staff, or even a paid performer who specializes in the art of telling stories. The goal of storytelling is to share the story on a personal level, providing a much more intensive aesthetic experience than reading the story on one's own. One of the other nice features about storytelling is that it is universal. It knows no age limits. Even adults are enthralled by a good storyteller! The art is found in almost all cultures. Storytelling allows the students to increase their vocabulary while exercising their imaginations. Stories can also provide an introduction to diverse cultures, especially those based on oral history.

One offshoot of storytelling, which demands a further step than committed listening skills, is creative dramatics. The school media center could sponsor a theater presentation, with professional acting, as one of its special events offerings, or it could coordinate a drama club for the purpose of experiencing the literature. Impersonating storybook characters is especially popular with younger students. Students of all ages enjoy participatory programs of this sort. They can also take the stories and compare them with other versions or other genres, and with contemporary stories (or even movies and television shows) to find similarities. The classic example is to compare *West Side Story* with *Romeo and Juliet*. The heroic characters and powerful themes that are the basis of many great classic novels are also found in many modern-day stories.

Literature provides much enjoyment. Its forces shape people's actions, and the quality of the characters provides common ties that unite people everywhere. The programming that the school library media center develops around literature helps students acquire lifelong skills that enable them to experience and become personally involved in literature.

Programming in the media center can have its challenging moments, but it is also a great deal of fun. Because such programs expose students to all sorts of new ideas, they must meet high expectations. Fresh ideas and enthusiastic presentations are important ways of engaging students. Furthermore, the programs will create a new appreciation of the school library media center.

Developing Partnerships to Support Special Events Programs

3

Special events are an important method of providing both informational and educational experiences for students. Although different strategies may be used to obtain specific learning goals than those used in the classroom, nonetheless, special events are part of the educational process. These programs should be entertaining and enjoyable for both the students and the staff. However, building programs into an already busy schedule is not necessarily easy. In fact, because they are out of the ordinary, special events programs can be incredibly demanding. Precautions must be taken to avoid putting additional stress on an already overextended staff. Flexibility is one key to avoiding potential frustrations. We must become comfortable with reorganizing and reprioritizing daily tasks so that we have both the time and the energy to fit these events into our schedule. Furthermore, we must move past fitting them in, to building other events around them instead. In addition, we must also develop alternative methods of accomplishing some of our daily tasks, as well as some of the components that will make our special events programs successful.

In order to proceed, it will become necessary to match the library media center's goals with the teaching goals of the school. Identifying these similarities will help you to begin implementing these programs through alliance relationships. Interdependence among those who share responsibility for the students' well-being will provide you with a means of extending the media center's capability of reaching out to students.

To effectively institute a program with partners, two primary considerations must be kept in mind. First, consider the possible benefits to each of the partners. Second, clearly define the roles and responsibilities of all the parties involved. Establishing mutual understanding between partners sets the stage for successful cooperation on the special event.

Other personnel within the school are the first allies to consider. The faculty will be cooperative if the program is designed to help meet some of the goals of the curriculum. The professional staff will appreciate that offering different programs will provide expanded learning opportunities to accommodate different learning styles. Basic day-to-day library services are usually delivered on a one-to-one basis. Programming, on the other hand, attempts to reach individuals through group experience. Therefore, adequate staffing must be available to supervise large groups and to assist the school media specialist in personalizing the learning for the students.

Other specialists in the school community are important partners as well. Reading specialists, school psychologists, and guidance counselors, among others, are useful allies. The art teacher and the industrial arts instructor can help to construct sets and produce graphics, and the home economics teacher might be able to assist with refreshments. In addition to helping on the day of the event, these people are also potential event co-planners. Through their work, too, you will hear of program ideas, and their network might also be able to put you in contact with program performers and presenters.

Another group of people who will be eager to assist are parents. Most schools have parent-teacher associations or organizations. They are natural supporters who may be willing to raise funds to pay for special events. Also, parents are often willing to volunteer their time to help plan, organize, and supervise. It is also valuable to remember that parents and extended families are a tremendous resource in themselves. They should be asked if they have special skills or talents that they would be willing to share. Often people do not give themselves credit for their knowledge or abilities or do not feel that what they do is special, so they may need some coaxing. However, your efforts will be greatly rewarded. You may discover individuals willing to share ethnic folklores and traditions or special skills and interests that will add a new dimension to everyday learning. In addition, funding special events becomes more manageable with this in-kind support, and it is almost impossible to duplicate their sincerity and authenticity. Students and family members benefit tremendously from exposure to these experiences, and also from the self-esteem that results from being involved. This is a technique that will work over and over again, because each school year will provide you with new students, families, and faculty to tap for assistance. In many ways, you have a source that renews itself. Take some time to investigate it!

Both businesses and not-for-profit support agencies are often interested in being good neighbors by donating to and volunteering in the schools. Before beginning to search for outside support, it is advisable to enumerate some of the benefits you will be able to offer these groups in return for supporting your media center. This list should be broad enough to attract a variety of supporters. However, careful thought should also be given to the significance of aligning the media center with a particular organization. Clearly, if a partnership is going to work, the partners must be comfortable with each other.

Many businesses are interested in giving something back to their communities, and they have different ways of expressing this interest. Some offer their employees the opportunity to volunteer some hours during the school day. Others have foundations that target their contributions in terms of specific priorities. Your public relations program, which should be operating on a consistent, ongoing basis, is a vital mechanism for gaining their support. Often businesses or groups make financial contributions or volunteer commitments based on past relationships with an institution and their knowledge of your performance and reputation. Private sector partners are more likely to assist with programs when they understand your goals. To attract private sector partners, you must clearly state your objectives and how you plan to achieve them. This gives them a firm, common-sense basis on which to make their decision to support a project. They need to know what you will be doing with their contribution and how this will benefit their image in the community.

How can you find organizations willing to support a special event? If you are aware of what goes on in your school's community, this is actually much easier to do than you might think. You can check standard reference tools such as *The Foundation Directory* or a statewide directory on your topic. Or you can use local newspapers to informally track the activities supported by area organizations. You will be able to develop a list of those who are known for their generosity, and what causes they support. In addition to being good neighbors, they, like you, are interested in the students' welfare. The students are the future work force, and it is advantageous for employers to have a labor pool of well-educated individuals who enjoy a good quality of life.

Some rules of etiquette should be followed once you have identified groups to contact. Begin by identifying the right person in the company—the one responsible for community relations. Call and set up an appointment. Most likely, you will be asked why you want to meet. Be prepared to give a thumbnail sketch of your idea.

Do your homework before you go to the appointment. You should have a written proposal outline that includes program goals and objectives, the number of students you will be reaching, the anticipated learning outcome, and how you plan to evaluate the program. You will usually be asked to assign dollar figures to the program so that the potential funder will be able to make a financial decision. The business may also request your marketing plan, or, in other words, how they will receive recognition for their support. You should be prepared to provide some answers—for example, acknowledging their contribution in a sample program flyer and booklet, including a paragraph about their support in a press release, allowing a company representative to attend the special event and talk with the students, or providing some form of recognition for the company to display in its corporate offices (a plaque is a good example). More will be said about these processes in Chapter 6.

Civic clubs and service organizations are another pool of possible partners for the school media center. The main purpose of many of these groups is to make a difference within the community. Again, they may have members among your faculty or parents' groups, thus making it easier for you to gain the cooperation of these groups. The local Chamber of Commerce is an important source of information about such organizations. Civic groups generally have priorities governing the types of programs they support. They may also supply volunteers to help with events.

Like businesses, these organizations will want to know how participating in your event will benefit them. Will someone from the school join their group? Will someone serve on a board? Will their sponsorship be recognized in print? It's best to be prepared for these questions when you first sit down with a representative of a potentially helpful organization.

In any case, flexibility and a willingness to compromise will make these partnerships function more smoothly. Without question, they take a great deal of nurturing, but truly it is worth all the effort when you see the enthusiasm with which your special events programs will be met.

Figures 3.1 and 3.2 offer practical procedures useful in developing coalitions with the various groups discussed above. They are not intended to be totally inclusive—you need to examine your program and change or adapt the questions to make the forms work for you. Keep in mind that their purpose is not to create more work for you, but rather to simplify the process of identifying potential partners, giving you more time to nurture those relationships.

The answers to the questions on these two checklists should begin to clarify the environment in which you will be developing alliances. If you are unable to answer some of these questions, or if you have found a great many negative responses, you will then have some direction on how to proceed. While initially frustrating, this process can start you on your way to successful partnerships.

Adults, even those with no children of their own, must participate in our schools to assure their success within our communities. With this support, the positive attitudes we will be able to build within the schools will be transferred to the work force later on, and will be there to nurture a new generation of learners.

Figure 3.1
Checklist for Developing Partnerships with Parents

1. Does your school media program recognize the difficulties posed by parents' work schedules?
2. What accommodations have been made to assist parents?
   Saturday media center hours
   Evening hours
   Other
3. Do you have adult reading materials on parenting available?
4. Do you have materials available to assist parents in working with their children on schoolwork?
5. Are parents involved in the day-to-day operation of your media center?
   How?
6. Are parents invited to become actively involved in a reading promotion for their children?
7. Are parents involved in current special activities such as field trips or read-aloud days?
8. Is there a schoolwide event that encourages families to socialize with staff?

Figure 3.2
Checklist for Developing Community Partnerships

1. Have local businesses and neighborhood community organizations ever been invited into the school on a school day?
   For what reason?
   How was the day evaluated?
2. Are library and school activities publicized in the local news media (both print and nonprint)?
3. What members of the school community have links to these businesses/organizations, either through employment or membership?
4. Are parents or faculty asked to *volunteer* information about their affiliations?
5. What are some of the primary causes that have been adopted by these businesses or organizations?

GETTING TO KNOW SCHOOL EMPLOYEES

The following list suggests ways to develop relationships with other individuals in the school. You will come to depend on their assistance and cooperation for special events programs.

- Call or write a note to all new school employees, introducing yourself and the media center.
- Participate formally in new employee orientation programs. Host them in the media center.
- Give presentations to the faculty (by department in larger schools) about the services of the media center. Discuss resources, including new technologies, that will help them with their work.
- Have a brochure available to distribute to all faculty, staff, and administration. You will probably need to prepare one with a different focus than the brochure designed for students.
- Be flexible. Bend the rules once in a while.
- Welcome suggestions for new procedures as well as for new materials.
- Be aware of what units are being taught. Design a "request sheet" that teachers can use to request materials, services, and bibliographies that fit in with their projects.
- Establish a media center advisory committee to assist in suggesting acquisitions and weeding of materials.
- Provide materials that teachers can use for bulletin boards and display in their classrooms.
- Provide all service with a smile. Smiles do not cost any more; they require very little effort and work wonders to get people to cooperate with you.

4
Raising Community Support for and Awareness of the Media Center and Its Programs

In order to be successful, special events programs need to have the support, both financial and emotional, of members of the entire community. The effectiveness of these programs is based, first of all, on the commitment and collaboration of those directly involved in promoting student learning. Second, the collaboration must extend beyond the walls of the school. Indeed, the local community and society in general have a vested interest in helping students, the taxpayers of tomorrow, succeed in school.

Students who are well educated and who have had exposure to the broadening experiences that special events provide grow up to be individuals who want to make contributions to their communities. Students should be encouraged to be partners as well as participants in special events. They learn wonderful organizational skills this way, as well as how to work well with other people—skills that they will bring with them to the workplace. In addition, these opportunities early in life create an appreciation for the arts, both visual and performing. The students become aware of the value of the arts and are predisposed to become lifelong supporters. This is one significant justification for supporting these events.

Partnership and collaboration are necessary to make these events happen. You will need financial support, and because special events are so labor-intensive, you will also need people to help out. Others are needed to help pull together all the details and perform all the tasks involved. Teamwork makes the job more manageable. It also serves to stimulate new ideas and fosters cohesiveness and effectiveness. Working together expands the resources and skills at your disposal, making it possible to carry out projects that would exhaust one individual. Partnership generates enthusiasm and energy.

It is natural for collaboration to develop between departments with interdisciplinary links. Teachers have the day-to-day responsibility of teaching students individually; on a broader scope, teachers and media specialists have the long-term task of educating students. For this long-term process, the two groups need to rely on each other, working together to coordinate special events. In addition to working within their own school, it is important for library media specialists to share ideas and offer joint projects with other media specialists in the school system. Working with parent-teacher organizations (PTAs or PTOs) and with parent groups also makes sense.

There are many ways to get people to collaborate on special events programs. The first step is to get people *into* your media center. One idea that has proven successful is holding a faculty meeting or a PTA meeting in the media center. Providing light refreshments for this type of event is appropriate and will make people feel at home. If you do this, make sure that the media center is in top-notch shape. Displays should be inviting, "housekeeping" details accomplished, and all personnel friendly and welcoming.

The next step is for the school library media specialist to begin an outreach program. The media specialist who wants to attract collaborative partners needs to have a very high profile in the community. You can achieve this by joining civic organizations, offering to participate in community committees and task forces (United Way, Gang Prevention, beautification projects, etc.), joining clubs and organizations of personal interest or ones that can help the library program, volunteering at events or festivals, and attending community events sponsored by other organizations. When people within the community see that you are interested in helping them achieve their goals, they are more likely to help you achieve yours. This reciprocal commitment is one of the most important elements in making this partnership work.

Commonly shared visions, goals, and objectives are important for cross-institutional activities. They constitute a dynamic force that will help you provide coordinated, quality programs and services. Many community institutions and organizations have goals and visions consistent with those of the educational system. These entities will make the best partners for your special events program process. The most obvious partner is the public library. Its mission of promoting lifelong learning carries on the work of the school system. The town parks and recreation departments are another good bet. Many of them have resources available to bring in special performers, and it might be possible for you to sponsor a joint event. Performing arts centers, symphonies, professional or amateur theater groups, or chorale groups are other possible partners. Museums and historical societies can coordinate their exhibits and events with media center offerings. All of these partnerships make it possible for the school media program to offer enhanced enrichment programs that will benefit the entire community and may have the added benefit of generating greater interest in the school media program.

In every partnership, both parties need to acknowledge their responsibilities. Specifics must be discussed at the very beginning of the relationship and must be agreed on by both parties. It is also appropriate to draw up some sort of written agreement between the parties. This preliminary work can prevent disappointment and confusion later on, because everyone knows what is expected of them. The agreement can take the form of a letter confirming a discussion, or it may be something more formal, such as a contract. Figures 4.1 and 4.2 are examples of informal and formal agreements.

Figure 4.1
Informal Agreement

Dan E. Jones, Director
Littletown Public Library
501 River Road
Littletown, CT 06000

Dear Dan:
    It was good to talk with you today. As we agreed on the phone, E. O. Mann Middle School will be delighted to exhibit the Library Week Photo Contest winners from April 20 through May 1. In return, we will supply our "Reading 'Round the World" exhibit for your summer reading programs in July and August.
    We will be ready to assist you in putting up the display on April 19. When we close for the summer on June 15, I will deliver our display to you.
    Thank you for having your staff do the press releases. It has been hard to get everything done with Ann on sick leave!
    It is wonderful to work with you.
Regards,

Mary Lee
School Library Media Specialist

Figure 4.2
Formal Agreement

Mary Lee agrees to lend the Littletown Public Library the "Reading 'Round the World" exhibit for the Littletown Public Library's Summer Reading Center.

Littletown Public Library agrees to take reasonable care to prevent damage to said exhibit. *Dan E. Jones* will return this exhibit to E. O. Mann School after September 5, 1996.

Mary Lee	*Dan E. Jones*
Library Media Specialist	Public Library Director
April 1, 1996	

When developing partnerships for major special events programs, it is very often necessary to write a synopsis of the program as you envision it. If you are looking for a partner to fund the project, it might be necessary to write a formal proposal. The following pages give an overview of how to go about it.

In addition to soliciting monies from private sources, there are many other grants from local, state, and federal sources that may be available to you.

Figure 4.3 is designed to help develop a one-paragraph summary to present to groups being approached for funding. It is also a very good checklist, because it forces the programmer or planner to think through the entire project.

Figure 4.4 gives a detailed outline of what information is needed to complete a proposal. It is very important that potential funders are given as much information as possible so that they can get a clear idea about the project.

Figure 4.3
Project Information Sheet

Project Name:

Project Date:

Project Audience:

Why? Why should the school media center undertake such a project? What is the primary goal? What current efforts are being made in the area? What unique contribution will this program make to your school?

What? What will your project accomplish within the school?

How? How will your project achieve its objectives?

Who? Who will do the project? You need to demonstrate that you will be able to complete your project. Your proposal should present a clear, logical progression of steps, showing how the components relate to each other. It is a good idea to specify the roles and responsibilities of the individuals who will be involved in implementing the project.

When? Your timetable is important. List deadlines. These should be benchmarks on the way to the event. Tell when the project will take place and how long it will last.

How Much? Estimate a budget. Be as specific as possible and project the expenses your project will incur.

Who Are You? Provide a complete statement about your organization, its mission, and whatever else you feel is important. Remember that performance precedes funding. Do not be shy about listing your accomplishments and letting people know what you are able to do! Confidence in your own abilities is important to make this process work.

Figure 4.4
Proposal Groundwork

I. Know All of Your Needs:
   A. Volunteers
      1. How many hours a week?
      2. What will they do?
      3. Who will train them?
      4. What are the long- and short-term needs?
      5. What recognition will they receive?
   B. In-Kind Services/Donations
      1. An amount of a product
      2. A cents-off coupon for an incentive
      3. Printing services
      4. Refreshments
   C. Cash Donations
      1. How much?
      2. What will dollars be used for?
         —Have a budget plan!
      3. What percentage of program budget are you requesting?
      4. Who else is giving money?
      5. How is school supporting these programs?
         a. Itemize staff hours and multiply by salary to indicate this as a contribution.
         b. Itemize the dollar value of all materials/equipment/supplies. (Two steps in items a. and b. show the school's commitment.)
      6. Be as specific as you can. Donors need to know what their dollars will fund.
II. Recognition—What Can They Expect?
   A. A photo in newsletter, newspaper
   B. A press story
   C. Company name on the program
III. Public and Private Thank-Yous
   A. Thank company's leadership.
   B. Thank all individuals who assisted with the project. Remember that success in special events programs is based on the people who are involved.
IV. Be Prepared
   A. Proposals of this sort are a natural outgrowth of the planning process. Clarity is essential. Those who are not involved in the school library media center on a regular basis will not necessarily understand your purpose.
   B. Have an evaluation plan. This helps funders measure the success of the project. It also shows your willingness to make adjustments to ensure that their contribution was used as cost effectively as possible.
V. Keep a Positive Attitude
   A. Break special events down into manageable pieces. It is the easiest way to identify needs and accomplish goals.
   B. Stick with the program and see it through. One success generates the energy to continue. Build on that momentum.

It is also important to interview potential partners to see if you share similar goals and if their reason for participating is consistent with yours. Completing a partner information sheet can be useful (see Figure 4.5). These forms can be filed for further use as well.

As we have seen, there are many reasons why it is important to involve the community in special events programs. Figure 4.6 suggests some ways to get the community and the public involved.

In conclusion, an ongoing public relations campaign is the foundation for special events programs. Establishing contacts throughout the year is time-consuming but they really pay off when you need them—they are a critical part of special events programs. Remember, your school library media center is in a position to show how important access to information can be—and the public relations surrounding your events program showcases the media center as an essential component of the school.

Figure 4.5
Partner Information Sheet

Partner Name:

Partner Address:

Partner Phone:
    Fax:
    E-Mail:

Giving History:
  Cash Donations:
  In-Kind Donations (Including Staff):
  Product Donations:

Special Interest/Focus of Partner:

Kind of Business/Organization:

Name of Principal Owners/Managers:

Company/Organization Contact Person:

Figure 4.6
Ways to Encourage Community Participation in Special Events

I. Run contests. These can be designed for different age levels. Entries can be displayed in prominent locations for others to see. They are especially valuable in promoting events.
    Photography
    Artwork

Figure 4.6 (continued)

        Essay
        Poetry
        Short Story
 II. Publish a community newsletter or magazine.
        Include contest winning pieces.
        Use it to inform.
        Use it to gather information.
        Use it to showcase your school.
III. Host an oral history project.
        Invite community members to visit school and tape their memories.
        Ask them to share their ideas with the students.
        Invite them to become volunteers and mentors for the students.
IV. Connect with others who consider education a priority.
        Church groups
        Ethnic groups/clubs
        Youth service agencies
        Social service agencies

5

Personnel Training and Strategies

Effective special events programming entails a broad range of expertise and professional skills. In addition to becoming proficient in the current practices of school librarianship, the individual who wants to offer special events must develop specialized skills to do them.

The actual assignment of responsibilities for planning, managing, and coordinating special events programs will vary according to the size and the staffing pattern of the school library media center. In many cases, the school library media specialist will also take on the additional title of "special events coordinator." In other cases, another individual in the school or a parent or community volunteer may take on this role. In any event, it is critical to the success of the project that there be one person to coordinate and oversee the entire event.

The special events programmer needs to be open-minded and committed to personal and professional growth. The skills needed include the ability to design programs from start to finish, to promote programs so that people will know about them, and to evaluate programs. All these tasks must be done taking into account students' abilities, ages, and developmental needs and interests. The goals of the media center and the school as a whole must also be considered.

A positive, nurturing attitude on the part of the school library media center staff is another vital factor in the success of special programs. Knowing how to attract volunteers and put them to good use is essential.

RECRUITING VOLUNTEERS

Volunteers are the backbone of most special events projects, no matter where they are held. School library media centers have an especially critical need for volunteer help. Because they are often understaffed, finding time to see to all the details a special events program entails is extremely difficult without extra help. When hosting an event, a great deal of fuss is often made about the performer. It would be wise to make the same amount of fuss over the volunteers, because it is truly these individuals who make the program possible. The special events coordinator who ties it all together depends heavily on the help of each volunteer. Everyone has a job to do, and doing it well is what makes the event successful.

Finding volunteers is not as difficult as one might think. Many people from all walks of life are willing to help out if they are asked. Just think for a moment about some of the reasons why people want to help, and you will be encouraged about finding volunteers. Some have children or grandchildren in the school and want to help because they see the event directly benefiting them. Others are retired and have more time to give now than when they were working. Others may want to help out to help themselves. Volunteering is a wonderful way to meet and socialize with others with similar interests. Many students want to help out as a form of community service; those thinking in terms of future careers may want to learn skills and gain work experience. The common thread is that they want to help. The coordinator's job is to see that these individuals are matched with the right task to keep them interested.

Do not overlook school personnel as a source of additional volunteers. These individuals are already trained to work with students. Their days are as busy as yours, though, so you had best reach them as early as possible in the planning process before they become overcommitted. In addition to their own services, take advantage of the contacts they have. They may not be able to offer time, but can refer others to you, or suggest sponsors.

While planning the event, the special events coordinator must make a running list of tasks and appropriate responsibilities. This is crucial if all of the details are to be handled properly. It simply is not enough to sign up people as helpers. They must be mobilized and motivated by careful nurturing and by letting them take ownership of their task. They need to be oriented and trained in order to cope with the task and any unexpected situations they might encounter.

Figure 5.1 shows a sample volunteer recruitment form that can be used to gather information.

The volunteer should be called by the special events coordinator within 48 to 72 hours after filling out the form. A brief discussion will fill in any empty or incomplete answers. The coordinator can then inform volunteers of meeting dates, when they will receive their assignment, and any training dates. This step is important, because a form by itself may not be enough to uncover unusual talents. A personal phone call can help you discover them. The phone interview can supplement informa-

Figure 5.1
E. O. Mann School Media Center Volunteer Recruitment Form

Name:

Address:

Phone no. (Home):
        (Business):

Best time to call:

Times available to work:

Are you a student?   yes__ no__ If so, what grade?

What experience/knowledge do you have about special events?

What type of tasks are you willing to do?
  typing
  fundraising
  developing posters
  getting sponsors
  producing newsletters
  helping with refreshments
  selling books, etc.
  picking up speaker at airport
  arranging for speaker reception
  helping with publicity
  watching classes/crowd control
  other

---

tion on the volunteer recruitment form. Possible areas to cover include the following:

- time and days available for work
- kind of work preferred
- kind of work least liked
- reason for volunteering (especially if community service is required for teens since they will need a letter of completion)

At this time you can also bring up the subject of a written agreement/commitment by the volunteer. There are various ways to handle this process. A follow-up letter can outline the main points of the conversation, or a more formal memo of agreement detailing the assignment and the time commitment required may be appropriate. Figures 5.2 and 5.3 give examples.

Figure 5.2
Confirmation Letter

E. O. Mann School Media Center

Mary Jo Barnes
22 Heather Lane
Lettertown, CT 06000

September 2, 1996

Dear Ms. Barnes:

It was a pleasure to speak with you today. I am delighted that you are going to chair the Sponsorship Committee for our "Meet the Author" week in April.

The first committee meeting is scheduled for September 16 at 2 P.M. in the E. O. Mann Media Center. At this time, you will meet the other subcommittee chairs and we will have a complete list of other volunteers ready for you. At this meeting, too, we will develop a meeting schedule, approximately one per month. We will need to have sponsorships in place by winter, so we know how much we can offer in terms of honoraria. As Chair, you can set the dates, time, and place for your meetings.

Thank you again for this generous offer of your time. It will be a pleasure to work with you.
Sincerely,

Mary Lee
School Media Specialist

Having this basic information on each volunteer is helpful when the time comes to match people with appropriate tasks. Keep in mind the following points when evaluating the suitability of a volunteer for a specific assignment:

- skills and experience
- knowledge of the library
- ability to fit in with staff
- other volunteer experience
- motivation for volunteering
- commitment letter

Developing a library volunteer packet for new recruits is a way to ensure that you haven't omitted any information a volunteer may need. You may want to include the following:

fact sheet on the library
calendar of upcoming events

Figure 5.3
Memo of Commitment

(Volunteer Name) agrees to serve as a volunteer for the "Meet the Author" week, April 1–8, at E. O. Mann Middle School. (Volunteer Name) agrees to chair the (Committee Name) and attend monthly update meetings as scheduled. In the event that (Volunteer Name) is unable to complete this assignment, said volunteer will provide adequate notice and recommend a replacement if possible.

(School Media Specialist Name) agrees to keep all volunteers informed of the progress of the committee and to provide all the background necessary to assist the volunteers in their tasks.

_____   _____
Volunteer Signature   School Media Specialist

---

   requirements for volunteer

   types of work available

   current list of staff and trustees/board of education members

   copies of any other necessary brochures

If you are recruiting volunteers from outside of the school community, it is important to set up a centralized information center for them. One effective way to do this is to post notices on a bulletin board. Also helpful is a handout that summarizes the policies of the school and the library media center relevant to volunteers. Include a floor plan of the media center and the school; indicate which facilities are open to volunteers (e.g., cafeteria) and any that are off limits. Also include schedules and any other information that will make their stay helpful. Copies of the handout are included in the volunteer packet and also are kept in the library media center.

TRAINING

Putting on special events may entail offering orientation and training sessions for volunteers. These sessions serve as a communications tool to make sure that everyone is knowledgeable about the event, and provide strategies to assist them in accomplishing their assigned tasks. Even if people are very comfortable working within the school's atmosphere, they may not have any experience at all in special events.

Training is the process of helping people acquire both an understanding of and expertise in performing specific tasks. It should also include an explanation of why a particular task is important. If people understand and appreciate why their task is necessary to the success of the program, they often perform them more efficiently. There are many methods of approaching this. You may even have to run separate sessions on particular tasks, for example, a session on how to approach potential sponsors, one on talking with the media, or one on managing school-age children. You cannot take it for granted that volunteers who have children know how to deal with large groups of them.

Training generally begins with an orientation session. A general orientation usually covers basic information as well as the goals, philosophy, and objectives of the organization. Orientation sessions may work by pairing a new volunteer with another who has done the task before. You may do a "walk-through" with a timed schedule so everyone knows what happens when. You absolutely should go over all emergency and evacuation plans, perhaps even simulating disasters so that people know how to respond. Figure 5.4 is a checklist of basic points to make during training. Figure 5.5 is a full-scale checklist for planning and evaluating a training program.

It cannot be emphasized enough that training must be carefully planned. Those in charge of training should find the following principles useful:

- Teach simple tasks first.
- Break tasks down into components.
- Use short teaching cycles, reinforced with practice and actual experience.
- Provide motivation and rewards for those who complete the training and then give their time to help the media center. (Example: Have a volunteer picnic after the event is over.)

Figure 5.4
Volunteer Training Checklist

- Purpose of the event and why it is being held
- Planning schedule
- Publicity schedule
- Orientation to the library and "House Rules" (parking, attendance, absences, emergency procedures, etc.)
- Details of the task
    Job description
    Time requirement
- Event walk-through
- Other

Figure 5.5
Event Coordinator's Training Checklist

I. Planning
   Is training needed?
   Who will need training?
   Who will do the training?
   How long should the training be?
   What will make the program run efficiently?
II. Purpose
   Why is the event being held?
   What learning is expected to take place?
   Is the project/event feasible?
III. How Many Volunteers Are Needed?
   What tasks will they do? (Give examples with short descriptions.)
   1. greeter: welcomes participants at door
   2. book sale coordinator: arranges with publisher to have author's works delivered; sets prices; coordinates volunteers; works with autographing logistics chair
   3. refreshment chair: plans after-event reception for participants, etc.
IV. Schedule of Orientation/Training Sessions
V. Evaluation Process
   Critique as you go along; you have to decide in advance what constitutes progress and reasonable success for the program.

SURVIVING EVENTS PLANNING

Most media specialists have to fit events planning in while fulfilling many other primary job responsibilities. Identifying key issues and using basic common sense are important survival strategies.

One basic survival technique is developing a sense of humor. This really means developing the ability to laugh at yourself. It means being flexible, rolling with the punches, and not getting upset. In addition, thorough, advance organization is essential so that there are not too many things to do at the last minute. Events always seem to run better if you are well rested and able to think clearly. That is simply because you can apply common sense and come up with a solution to a problem rather than panicking because you are overtired. Murphy's Law (anything that can go wrong will go wrong) is not so threatening when you have this attitude. The meticulous planning process discussed earlier will also help you overcome things that go wrong.

A few other tips are very useful in events planning. First of all, do not be afraid to ask questions. The only "stupid" question will be the one you don't ask! Ask them of performers, of volunteers, of anyone who has hosted special events—not just librarians or school media specialists. Never assume anything. If you think you forgot something, you probably did. If you think that someone else has done something but don't know, they probably haven't.

Put everything in writing. There are many good reasons for this. First, if you write it down, you have a better chance to remember it. Second, when things are in writing, it is clear to the planner and to the volunteers what is to be done and who is to do it. Keep lists, and cross out things as they are completed. This helps the memory process and has the added benefit of giving you a sense of accomplishment as you cross them out.

Knowing your audience is critical to success. Being familiar with the likes and dislikes of the student population, combined with creativity and attention to detail, is a strategy that will make your event successful.

Planning must always center around those who will participate in the special events programs. Always keep in mind the concepts you want the students to learn, and why. You should ask yourself if the events foster critical and creative thinking, and if the learning experience will help develop conceptual understanding. All programs should foster good learning attitudes.

Last but not least, be a stickler for quality. Don't take shortcuts that will affect the quality of the event. If you want excellence, chances are you are going to have to pay for it. If the budget is constraining you, you may have to design your program to work around it. You may need to find ways to supplement the budget, or even be very clever at cutting costs in ways that won't show.

Finally, take the time to enjoy your event. Yes, you have responsibilities during the event, but if you have done your homework and have worked hard to organize and train volunteers, you will have the time to enjoy it. Satisfaction at a job well done is the best motivation to get out and mobilize for a future event!

Here are some more hints for working with volunteers on special events:

- People who feel that they have some say in how they perform their tasks are more likely to remain committed to the process and may come up with innovative ways of getting things done.
- Teamwork means having critical control points. Choose "captains" and know the strengths and weaknesses of each team.
- Choose experienced committee heads/captains and pair them with less-experienced people.
- Build a "spirit" for the event by investing one's own time and by communicating on all levels.
- Responsibilities must be clearly delineated and volunteers supported by the coordinator.

- Remain flexible, open-minded, and willing to experiment and take risks.
- Caring and competent leaders set the example for caring and competent staff.
- Have faith in your own management skills. You will gain confidence as you gain experience and will also learn to anticipate possible problems and what you will be able to do about them.
- Learn not to worry about things that you cannot control. Do have backup plans, extra volunteers, and solutions for problems and issues that you can control.
- How the coordinator deals with a problem sends important signals to others. Learn to keep a cool exterior even if the butterflies are fluttering inside.

6
Developing Promotional Materials for Special Events

All library media programs should maintain a very visible profile within their schools on a regular basis. This is accomplished most efficiently through a solid public relations plan. This plan must include the best ways to reach the school community with information regarding the resources and services of the library media center, and it should offer an alternative perspective to the old stereotype of the library as a room of books. For special events, the library media specialist will benefit greatly from the support of powerful groups in the school—especially the administration, faculty, and other support staff. This support is gained over time, as the media specialist effectively communicates that the media center's goals are consistent with the goals and the objectives of the school. Such support is essential if the media center is going to be involved in special events programs.

Marketing activities are related to and relevant to the management procedures of the media center. These are two-way activities. The media center uses them to evaluate attitudes about the media center, and also to develop plans and procedures to increase the understanding and the acceptance of the organization. Good public relations is based as much on listening as on creating publicity tools that will have a positive influence on people's attitudes. This savvy public relations approach is the groundwork for promoting any specific event.

Spreading the word about programs is important. You want to do this so that potential participants know what is going on and how they can become involved. It would be unfortunate if after the event you hear, "I would have come or helped, but I didn't know about the program."

Analyzing your public relations strategy is a good starting point. Figure 6.1 gives one example of how to approach the task. After completing your

Figure 6.1
Public Relations Analysis Worksheet

The program: _____

Target audiences: _____

Media: _____

Media outlets: _____

Unique characteristics of the target audiences: _____

Support groups (yours): _____

Support groups (theirs): _____

What's been done before to inform/educate/motivate targets in this area: _____

What's in it for the target—stress these points in our communications: _____

Best time to promote to the target: _____

analysis, share it with everyone involved in the project. Come to a consensus about the facts, then get started on strategy development, budgeting, deciding on a time frame, and so on. Add or delete from this analysis, but keep it to a single page if possible.

When planning events, you must give some thought to the kinds of internal and external publicity that you will have to do to attract wider attention.

Posters are one item that can be used both inside and outside the school. Numerous computer programs are available to help design posters, making the task both easy and inexpensive. There are also companies that produce paper products that are different and attractive-looking, and the photocopying process makes this truly an inexpensive way to reach numerous audiences.

Book displays and three-dimensional exhibits can also be used to call attention to upcoming programs. They are good attention getters, attracting browsers and presenting materials to users in manageable quantities. These should be accompanied by bibliographies of selected books, articles, AV materials, and computer software to give the patron further choices. In addition to displaying these materials in the media center, they can be put in strategic community locations if the goal is to attract an outside audience. The public library is a natural site, as might be the post office, a shopping mall, and so on.

USING PRINT MEDIA

Press releases are another useful publicity method. The content and the timing of the release should reflect the goal of the publicity. For example, if the intent is to have community members attend the event, the press release needs to appear early enough to provide notice so that people can plan accordingly. If the intent is to inform the public of what is happening in the school, not to invite them to attend, the release can appear at any time, even after the event, accompanied by a photo. Depending on the scope of the event, more than one release may be appropriate, spaced over the course of a few weeks or even months. Background and biographical information about speakers or performers, as well as details about the event, should be included in the text.

For gala events, or events where a famous person will be performing, you might want to consider assembling a press kit to provide an overview of the entire event. It can be sent to local newspapers, radio, and television stations. The kit includes a statement about program goals and objectives, a black and white photograph, and a poster. Sometimes other promotional items such as bookmarks or buttons are included (see Figure 6.2). The content of the press kit varies with the specific needs of a program. All of the items listed will not be necessary for every program.

Press releases and press kits are not difficult to develop. They are most effective when they present the facts clearly and simply. Editors receive many, many releases. To attract their attention, be sure to follow some basic rules when you send a release. It will make their work easier and improve your chances of placement.

Figure 6.2
Checklist of Suggested Items for a Press Kit

- Attractive folders to hold all materials
- Business card of school media specialist
- Press release
- Camera-ready artwork of logo
- Publicity photo
- Public service announcement
- Bookmark or camera-ready bookmark for photocopying
- Promotional button
- Bibliography of author's works (especially useful if author visit is the special event)
- Poster
- Schedule of event
- Copy of author's book for review purposes
- Map of the facility

The release should have a professional appearance. Always submit typed copy, double spaced, on one side of the paper only. Use the school's name and address as the heading, or use letterhead. A contact person should be identified with a phone number, a fax number, and even an E-mail address. Give a release date. This should be in keeping with the publication's specific guidelines. Use a title that captures the content of the story. This, too, encourages the editor to read it. Follow the advice of journalists. Answer the questions who, what, when, where, why, and how in the first paragraph, with additional information in the following paragraphs. Assume that the reader knows very little about the subject; this will help you communicate what he or she needs to know. See Figure 6.3 for an example. Finally, proofread every word, or have a colleague do it for you.

Written releases are effective and economical. In order to ensure that the local press uses them, it is helpful for the school media specialist to make personal contact with the editors. Again, proper planning comes into play; long before the need arises, you should make an appointment with the local press and identify the person who will be covering the library. Ask what requirements or formats the paper has for materials that you will be

Figure 6.3
Sample Press Release

E. Z. Middle School
123 Center Road
Anytown, CT 06000
telephone:
fax:

Contact: M. J. Smith
   ext. 83
   mjsmith@con.com

FOR IMMEDIATE RELEASE   8–29–96

E. Z. Middle WELCOMES NEW STUDENTS

   School media specialist M. J. Smith invites all new E. Z. Middle School students to a pizza party on Tuesday, September 3, at 3 P.M. in the library media center. Local author and E. Z. Middle graduate Amee Low will be on hand to visit with students and sign copies of her new book, *When I Was 13, I Was Lucky!*
   Parents are also invited to this event, which is sponsored by Andy's Pizza Plus. There is no charge, but please call E. Z. Middle for reservations or further information.

---

sending, and how much lead time is necessary. Papers with a small circulation are more apt to cover library news. In cities with larger papers, the emphasis is usually on national news, but there is almost always one section of the paper that deals with local news. In addition, don't overlook neighborhood papers, foreign language newspapers, or other special interest papers. Depending on the program you want to promote, these papers can help you reach a specific audience.

Finally, in some cases follow-up press releases on events that have already occurred may well be worthy news items. These are often accompanied by a photo taken at the event and serve to inform the community about what has happened.

USING BROADCAST MEDIA

Today's world is tuned to radio and television, so it is to your advantage to use these media for public service messages. Coverage of actual events, too, can make an interesting news story.

One of the major differences between print resources and broadcast sources is the depth of coverage. Broadcasts can usually cover only the highlights, so a release directed to a radio or television station should be short and written so that the reporter can read it as a script. It should be written in simple sentences, using descriptive words. The first few words must get the attention of the listener.

Station managers or news directors are usually responsible for the decision to air a release, so it makes good sense to contact them just as you would print editors. Ask the same questions: What format do they prefer? and who, what, when, where, and why? It is also important to familiarize yourself with who their audience is and the kind of programming they offer. As a service, many stations broadcast community calendars where basic information is listed.

Public service messages for radio cover about 2.5 words per second; those for television use fewer, about 2 words per second, because viewers are using more than one sense at a time. This gives you an idea of why you must convey your message concisely. Before sending it out, practice it on someone else, or record it. Figure 6.4 shows a sample public service announcement (PSA).

Figure 6.4
Sample Public Service Announcement

E. Z. Middle School
123 Center Road
Anytown, CT 06000
telephone:
fax:

Contact: M. J. Smith
        ext. 83
        mjsmith@con.com

E. Z. MIDDLE SCHOOL WELCOMES NEW STUDENTS

Will you be a new student at E. Z. Middle this September? Come to the pizza party at the library media center, Tuesday, September 3, at 3 P.M. Meet fellow newcomers and Amee Low, author of *When I Was 13, I Was Lucky!* Pizza compliments of Andy's Pizza. Call the school for further information.

Air time: 20 seconds
Words: 50

Cable television provides another opportunity for promotion. Events or series of events can be broadcast on cable as well. Through the public access channel, the media center will be able to air shows (videos) that they produce with the school's equipment. Cable companies usually offer possibilities for production as well. A show hosted by students is an example of the kinds of activities that are possible. The students can interview one another about books they have read. Recommendation by peers is one of the best advertisements of all. They can also interview the media specialist or other faculty members about an upcoming event. There is one word of caution. The interviewers need to be prepared. Sample questions, some props to hold up to the camera, and note cards with announcements will make the presentations flow better. A dress rehearsal is also a very good idea.

OTHER TOOLS

It is obvious that no single method can provide all of the promotional coverage that your school library media center may need. Making promotions work for you will require a variety of techniques for the different programs and services you are offering. The key element in all these methods is keeping the media center in the public eye. This is done by continually fostering relationships with the community. Public relations activities do more than encourage use of services or attendance at events. Telling the media center's story on a steady basis builds goodwill and support, elements without which programs will not succeed.

One of the most effective tools a school library media center can use is a newsletter. It can be distributed throughout the school and can also be sent out to others in the community at large. It can be used to introduce new materials and services, to inform people of policies and procedures, and to highlight special events. The best newsletters are entertaining as well as informative. Here are some guidelines to follow for producing a newsletter:

- Give the newsletter a catchy title.
- Use clip art and colored paper to make it attractive.
- Use short, concise sentences.
- Use humor.
- Keep layout simple.
- Use plenty of white space to make it easy to read.
- Use boxes to call attention to key items.
- Make sure your "master" is clear, and dark enough to copy.
- Ask other faculty to be guest columnists.
- Ask students to be guest editors/columnists.
- Have a space in which to publish comments sent in by readers.

Flyers are an inexpensive way of getting a message across. They can be made in-house easily with several computer programs and adapted for different ages or groups. Flyers can be used as preliminary announcements (see Figure 6.5), or geared to a specific group (see Figure 6.6). Or they can be part of an overall calendar of events (see Figure 6.7). With some graphics added, the flyer format can be an inexpensive but extremely effective way to reach many people.

Here are some suggestions for producing effective flyers and brochures:

- Decide whether to make a flyer or a brochure based on how much information you need to convey.
- Put yourself in the reader's place. What do you need to know about the subject?

Figure 6.5
Sample Preliminary Announcement

SAVE THIS DATE

TUESDAY, SEPTEMBER 3

3 P.M.

E. Z. MIDDLE SCHOOL LIBRARY MEDIA CENTER

BE THERE!

Figure 6.6
Sample Flyer

ATTENTION ALL NEWCOMERS!

COME TO THE
LIBRARY MEDIA CENTER
TUESDAY, SEPTEMBER 3
3 P.M.

MEET OTHERS WHO ARE
NEW TO
E. Z. MIDDLE

Figure 6.7
Media Center Monthly Calendar

E.Z. Middle School Media Center Calendar
SEPTEMBER 1996

SUNDAY	MONDAY	TUESDAY	WEDNESDAY	THURSDAY	FRIDAY	SATURDAY
1	2 Labor Day School Closed	3 3–5 P.M. Pizza Party for Newcomers	4	5	6	7
8	9 Media Center Open until 4	10	11	12 Media Center Open until 4	13	14
15	16	17 Media Center Open until 4	18	19 Media Faculty Meeting 3:30–5:30 P.M.	20	21
22	23 Media Center Open until 4	24	25	26 Media Center Open until 4	27	28
29	30					

- What kind of visual impact do you want to create? It is important to use a familiar logo or graphic so that the item is immediately identified as being from the media center.
- What will best serve your purpose—photos, illustrations, design, etc.?
- Choose a layout plan that reflects your budget.
- Have you included all necessary details—who, what, when, where, why, how?
- Make a draft and share it with a few people who are not involved in the project. Do they get the message you want to convey? Have them proofread it too.
- Release and distribute them in a timely fashion so that people can respond.

DISTRIBUTING PUBLICITY

Depending upon the nature of the event, you will need to use various information formats to reach different groups. Your mailing list might include public librarians, community arts organizations and museums, PTA leaders, Boys and Girls Clubs, and book and music stores. You may want to set up displays at the local library, in merchants' windows, and at the senior citizens' center. You might send a complimentary copy of a book or tickets to reviewers and editors, make personal visits to classrooms to speak about the event, and put bulletin boards up in locations in the school other than the media center.

In addition, you can involve both the students and the faculty in designing and making promotional materials. Art and graphics programs within the school are a valuable resource for this. Posters don't need to be printed professionally—some of the best ones are made by the students. Button-makers are available commercially as well, and students love to use them. Balloons, billboards, and t-shirts might also be appropriate choices for particular programs. In any case, capitalize on the unique qualities and resources that you have available and put them to good use.

In addition, the school library media specialist should seek assistance from outside the school. Perhaps a graphics or advertising firm in town would help with design on a pro bono basis. Local papers have design teams in their display and advertising departments; printing companies or businesses with their own printing facilities may offer to print materials for you. It is essential to use all of the resources at your disposal to convey your message. Remember, public relations is really what the media center is about—providing information. So don't be afraid to find new ways to promote your library media center and your programs.

Figure 6.8 outlines the publicity manager's duties and a sample time frame. It is intended to provide a working time line that the publicity manager can use to release information on the event in a timely fashion.

Figure 6.8
Sample Publicity Manager's Schedule

Timing	Task
5–12 months prior to event	• Recruit and meet with planning committee. • Use theme to develop event name and logo. • Outline audience characteristics. • Publish date in member newsletter calendar.
3–5 months prior	• Meet monthly with committee. • Figure preliminary budget with treasurer. • Ask performers for biographies and photos. • Design publicity strategy and materials. • Draft press releases, fact sheets, etc. • Shoot photos and video public service announcements. • Ask for bids from printers.
2–3 months prior	• Meet monthly with committee. • Coordinate program with program manager. • Drop off originals at printer. • Pick up publicity from printer. • Send publicity to organization newsletters. • Address and mail invitations. • Deliver publicity to external media.
1–2 months prior	• Meet monthly with committee. • Create ads; deliver with payments. • Prepare display windows and on-site banners. • Set up windows and banners as permitted.
1 week prior	• Meet with committee. • Arrange for press tickets; reserve seating. • Collect press kits and name tags for media. • List media personnel for registrars. • Distribute posters.
1 day prior	• Use checklist to organize and pack up materials if the event is not in the library. • Poster important sites again. • Get some sleep (well, at least try).
EVENT DAY	• Greet media personally. • Schedule instant interviews. • Take photos. • Set up press room with publicity kits.
1 day after	• Clip all media mentions; send thank-yous. • Thank all of your volunteers. • Make notes on event evaluation. • Rest and recover.
2–4 weeks after	• Meet with committee for comment session. • Implement evaluation techniques.

7

Keys to Making Programs Successful

Your skill at coordinating special events increases as you gain experience. The more you do, the more you learn about managing them. You will learn what works and what not to repeat. If you are organized, you should not be afraid to try something new.

The elements of the planning process for programs and special events discussed in earlier chapters are key checkpoints in ensuring their success. As you work on the program's content, remember that you are trying to achieve specific learning goals; the measurement and evaluation process is the built-in checkpoint for this. Cost control and promotion of the program are the other checks. If costs are getting out of control, perhaps your program design is unrealistic. The promotional activities undertaken should be sufficient to provide information about the event, but the effort involved should not outweigh the effort devoted to program design. If it does, you have spent your time and money on promotion, not on the event.

Program redesign is needed if at any time within the planning cycle staff members determine that one or more program elements are not effective. Redesign involves changing, adapting, or restructuring a forthcoming event to ensure its success based on ongoing evaluation.

THE EVALUATION PROCESS

The process of evaluating special events programs begins with the initial planning and continues until the program is totally completed. Continuous evaluation is important; if you wait until the end, it may be too late to make changes, and experience has shown that little changes can make all the difference in the overall success of a program. In order to keep special events programs on the right planning course, it is important to use an interim or progress report system. This may be done through group meetings, where people talk about how things are going and what changes are needed. Often someone not directly involved in a particular aspect of the planning can see things more objectively and come up with a solution to a problem. Posting charts, graphics, and checklists for all committee members to see is another good technique to use. Ongoing communications, perhaps in the form of a newsletter, can also help keep your program on track.

A final report that evaluates an event comprehensively is critical to the credibility of the program. It should be structured to help you determine the true value of the event and if it met the original objectives. A post-event meeting to rehash what worked and what did not is one way to accomplish this. In any event, it is crucial to ask for criticism, both positive and negative.

The evaluation process needs to take into consideration how the event or program helped the students learn. Establishing a measurable learning objective at the outset provides you with a measurable goal for this purpose. Depending on the scope of the program, you may need to design several different types of evaluations to measure the achievement level of the students by grade or age. Clearly, from this process, you will be able to measure their learning against the expectations that you had for the program.

Evaluation is a process that allows you to learn from what is happening; it lets people know what happened; and it makes you think about how all of it worked. Meeting expectations with one program and communicating this fact is the first step toward another program. In order to fully evaluate a program's success, it is important to take into consideration input from the audience and the performers as well as from the committee.

Performer and Audience Input

When evaluating a program in which outside performers or presenters participated, it is useful to ask for their comments. Ask them to evaluate the contact process you employed; how you stated your requirements for the program; and how you stated the learning objective. In addition, ask for logistical feedback. This includes such questions as, Was our contract clear? Were the directions helpful? Was the target audience discussed? Was the room set up in accordance with your request? Was all the necessary equipment in place? Was the staff helpful, particularly in unexpected situations? It is perfectly acceptable to ask performers to provide you with this information and to offer any additional comments that they feel would be helpful to you in the future.

What to ask the audience about the event will, of course, vary according to the grade level of the students. In an elementary school, it might be useful to ask teachers to hold a class discussion after the event and summarize the results for you. At the high school level, it is appropriate to have students complete a written evaluation form (see Figure 7.1 for an example). Appropriate questions might include the following: What was the most memorable part of the program for you? What facet of the program did you like least of all? Did you take part in any of the related activities or note displays that were done in coordination with the program? And finally, if attendance was not required, How did you hear about the program? and What persuaded you to attend? Also take this opportunity to request suggestions from them and ask whether they would be interested in participating in planning future events.

Figure 7.1
Sample Program Evaluation Form

Choose the term that best describes your opinion and write the corresponding number in the blanks below.

	Excellent	4
	Good	3
	Fair	2
	Poor	1

1. Publicity: How accurately did it describe the program? _____

2. Content: How informative was it? _____

3. Presentation: How interesting was it? _____

4. Format: How well suited was it to the program? _____

Things you liked about the program:

_____

_____

Things that could be improved:

_____

_____

Suggestions:

_____

_____

Please return to the School Library Media Center.

The Final Report

The school media specialist or the person who planned the program should do a thorough evaluation process that is summarized in a final report. In order to be true to the curriculum and to the goals set down during the planning process, the most important questions to answer are, Were the learning objectives met or not? How or why not? Notes should also be made on every facet of the program. An evaluation of outside performers is one component. The program planner should determine if they met the obligations of their contract; if they arrived on time; if they were well organized; and if they had all of the necessary equipment, handouts, and so on, that they said they would arrive with. It is important to note if they were prepared, how they dealt with the audience, and if their work was helpful in meeting the learning objective. The planner also needs to evaluate the facilities and logistics. Did the room setup work? Was all equipment in good working condition? How were crowds managed? Was security an issue?

If there were accompanying displays, exhibits, or activities, how were they used? Were they effective? Were the activities age-appropriate and geared to ability levels? Were there any activities that could not be managed?

In most cases, it is appropriate to evaluate programs in terms of cost-effectiveness, the number of people in attendance, and the value of the program for those who attended it. All of this must be balanced against staff time and effort and the expenditure of resources.

The effectiveness of the public relations effort must also be measured. The number of people who attend an event is just one indicator of the effect that your efforts had. You should also look at media coverage and letters of thanks from those who attended and listen for comments throughout the school and the community. Very often people complain when there is a problem, but unfortunately many do not take the time to congratulate you on an outstanding special event. You will need to train yourself for signs that tell you that it was good!

Figure 7.2 shows the kinds of data and feedback that should be included in a final report. The report serves as a permanent record of the event and documents what went well and what did not. And, most of all, it should be useful to someone else who may want to offer the program in the future. The recordkeeping should not be so cumbersome that it takes over your time. Remember, the purpose is to be helpful. Keep it simple and short, but keep it accurate!

The following pages contain detailed recommendations and steps to follow when planning special events programs. Paying attention to these small details will help make your program a success.

Figure 7.2
Sample Final Report Form

Program Title:	Simple title of the event
Program Description:	One to two paragraphs about the program
Program Objectives:	State the reason/purpose for planning the program and summarize any learning objectives
Date of Program:	For future reference
Time of Program:	Evaluate the time of the event (during school day, after school, evening)
Audience Characteristics:	The grade/age of those attending; the size of the audience; audience response (enthusiastic, uninterested, responsive, bored)
Program Resources:	Who presented the program? How was it received? What other resources/materials were used?
Staff:	Who was in charge of organizing the event? How many other people assisted? (paid and volunteer)
Suggested Improvements/ Comments:	What worked and can be repeated? What didn't work? How was the content?
	If the program accomplished what you wanted it to, was success due to the performer? Or if it didn't, was failure due to a lack of content? Be specific.
Recommendations for Future Programs:	Would you do this program again? Why or why not? Are there elements that you would change in future programs?
Appendix:	Include samples of all materials and forms used to organize the event, for example, flyers, bookmarks, posters, news clippings, programs, and actual photographs of the event. A letter of thanks and appreciation can also be included.

FOCUSING ON LEARNING OBJECTIVES

Writing Learning Objectives for Special Events

If your goal is to enhance learning through special events, it is important to think through the desired learning objectives as you would for any other lesson. They should contain as much detail as possible. Here are some simple rules to follow, especially when the events are geared to the curriculum.

- Learning objectives should describe intended outcomes.
- Learning objectives should be stated in behavioral terms. These describe what the learner will be doing when demonstrating achievement of the objective.
- Learning objectives should describe what the students are expected to learn and what method(s) would be used to evaluate their progress.
- Learning objectives for an entire program of instruction consist of specific statements.

Selecting Appropriate Programs to Meet Learning Objectives

Ask yourself the following questions to help determine if a particular program is appropriate for the learning objective that you have in mind.

1. Is the presentation method suited to the objectives?
2. Does it lend itself to knowledge, skill, or attitude acquisition?
3. Might it produce learning of more than one type?
4. How much time will it take?
5. How much space will be needed?
6. What special equipment/activities will be needed?
7. Will it challenge the knowledge of participants?
8. Are special skills required of the staff? Are they competent in them?
9. Is the method appropriate for the participants, and is the staff comfortable with it?
10. Does the method call for activity or passivity on the part of the participants?
11. Can we afford the method?
12. Are there any reservations about having this method incorporated into a special event?

The project information sheet in Figure 4.3 on page 52 also provides a series of questions that should be asked and answered to determine the objectives of the special event.

Resources to Support Special Events

The media specialist can call on a wide range of resources to support special programs (see Figure 7.3). This list of different types of media provides choices that can be utilized for special events instruction.

Figure 7.3
Checklist of Media Types for Special Events Instruction

Printed Media	**Audiovisual Media**	**Realia**
Books	Visuals	Plants
Nonfiction	Transparencies	Animals
Literature	Slides	Rocks and minerals
Reference books	Filmstrips	Artifacts
Fiction	Film/video	**Miscellaneous Media**
	Microfilm/fiche	
Ephemera	Audiotapes	Games
Pamphlets	Compact disc	Laboratories
Clippings		Puppets
Documents	**Computer Media**	Kits
	Drills	Bulletin boards
Graphics	Databases	Puzzles
Pictures	CD-ROMs	Dolls
Charts	Simulations	Models
Graphs		Dioramas
Maps		
Globes	**Human Resources**	
Paintings	Resource person	
	Voice	
Periodicals	Body language	
Magazines		
Newspapers		

SELECTING AND CONTRACTING WITH A SPECIAL EVENTS PROVIDER

You will want to bring in individuals from outside your school system to provide performances, lectures, and activities as part of your special events program schedule. The following pages will assist you in working through the mechanics of selecting and hiring them. The list below can be used as a starting point:

Things to consider before looking for a provider:
- Type of program appropriate
- Content of program
- Learning objectives
- Characteristics and size of group
- Time allotment
- Your budget

Things to know about your provider:
- Presentation skill and ability
- Usual methods of presentation
- Experience with groups similar to yours
- Reputation
- Credentials and competency in field

Things to discuss in initial contact:
- Be clear about the results you want
- Ask provider to describe his/her style
- Negotiate for the presentation you want
- Ask if it is possible to preview a performance already scheduled
- Negotiate fee/honorarium

Things to follow up in writing after initial contact:
- Restatement of phone conversation
- Schedule/time commitment
- Fee/honorarium
- Facility and equipment needs
- Any other details

Included are a sample letter to a program provider (Figure 7.4) and a contract form (Figure 7.5). Before entering into an agreement, be sure you have the authority to do so. It may have to be signed by the principal or another individual in the school system.

Following Up on Contracts

To ensure that the program is successful, it is important that the program planner follow up on the features of the contract. Both the school and the performer must have a clear understanding of what is expected of them. The responsibility for making sure that this happens rests with the school library media specialist.

The following suggestions should be helpful in this process:

1. Make sure that you provide the performer with all appropriate information about the audience—grade levels, special learning needs, size, etc.
2. If there are any changes in plans after the contract is signed, be sure to talk with the performer and make any necessary adjustments to the agreement.
3. Make sure you agree on the learning outcomes and the methods of the presentation.
4. Follow up on any equipment or special needs. Make sure they are in place for the event.
5. As a courtesy, call the performer a few days or a week before the event.
6. Follow up to make sure payments are made when promised. Include a thank-you note, any press clippings, or remarks that would be helpful to the performer for future performances.

Figure 7.4
Sample Correspondence with Provider

E. O. Mann Middle School
2 North First Street
Littletown, Conn. 06000
Telephone:
Fax:

Mr. Jack Lincoln
100 Painted Lane
Baytown, R.I. 05050

Dear Mr. Lincoln:

I am delighted that you have agreed to speak at our Annual Reading Olympics Opening Day Ceremony. Our students are very familiar with your books, and we are sure they will be motivated by your presentation.

I am enclosing our contract for your signature. The details of our October 23 event are contained in it.

As we discussed on the phone, your presentation should be aimed at our seventh and eighth graders. There will be two separate assemblies, one and a half hours long each. There are 123 seventh graders and 146 eighth graders.

Since you will be driving, we have enclosed a map and directions to the school. When you arrive, please go to the main office. Our secretary, Rose Reyonds, will meet you and call me. Lunch and dinner will, of course, be provided.

If you decide to stay overnight, please let us know. It would be our pleasure to make the necessary arrangements.

We are grateful that you have accepted our request to kick off this program. Please let us know if there is anything else you require for your visit.
Sincerely,

Mary Lee
School Library Media Specialist

Figure 7.5
Sample Contract

Program/Event Confirmation Form

Performer: (name)
             (address)
             (phone number)

Please complete and sign both copies. Keep one for your records. Return the other one to the E. O. Mann School, Mary Lee, School Library Media Center,

Figure 7.5 (continued)

2 North First Street, Littletown, Conn. 06000 within 5 days. Please include publicity photo and your resume for publicity purposes.

This agreement is made [date], by and between E. O. Mann School and [Performer's name].

Let it be known that E. O. Mann School hires [Performer] on the terms and conditions below:

Performances will be in the E. O. Mann School Auditorium, 2 North First Street, Littletown, Conn. 06000

Date of performance:

Starting time(s) and Durations: [insert performance time(s) and length of performance(s)]. Performer will arrive at least 30 minutes before the scheduled performance time. If said performer does not arrive on time, there is no guarantee that the program will take place or that the performer will be paid.

Compensation agreed upon:

Payable To: Payment will be made to [insert performer's name] by E. O. Mann School, Town of Littletown, within two weeks after the above performance date.

Special Provisions: [specify who will provide equipment, performing area requirements, agreement for sale of printed and/or recorded materials before and/or after the performance, etc.]

If performer is unable to perform any engagement as herein provided by acts of God, illness, physical disability, government action or court orders, labor disputes, strikes, insurrection, riot, transportation failure, or any cause of a like of similar nature, then the parties shall be relieved and discharged of any obligation stated in this agreement.

E. O. Mann School agrees not to broadcast, televise, tape, or reproduce by any device whatsoever the performance(s) and not to permit any other party to do so except where written permission has been granted by the performer in advance.

_____   _____
Performer's Signature   E. O. Mann School
                                                           Mary Lee, Library Media Specialist

ELEMENTS OF A BUDGET FOR SPECIAL EVENTS

Needless to say, financial resources are required to put special events together. It is a good idea to do a projected budget at the outset of the program so that you can be clear about how much money is needed. This is especially useful in getting support from outside of the school, both in terms of dollars and in-kind support. The following list can be used as a guide.

Revenue Sources
- Line item in budget
- Advertising in program
- Grants
- Donations
- In-kind services

Expenses

Program
- Speaker, presenter fee
- Room rental/overtime fees
- Equipment rentals
- Speaker meals/lodging
- Speaker transportation

Promotion
- Printing
- Postage
- Photographer
- Advertising

Exhibits
- Decorating
- Materials

Administration
- Photocopying
- Telephone
- Supplies
- Postage

Other
- Gratuities/gifts
- Miscellaneous

GUIDELINES FOR A SUCCESSFUL SCHOOL LIBRARY MEDIA CENTER PUBLIC RELATIONS PROGRAM

Public relations is one of the foundations of success (see discussion in Chapter 6). Here are some general guidelines to keep you on target.

1. Develop a policy about the role of the school library media center in education. This must become a part of the teaching philosophy of your school, understood by all teachers, staff, and administration.
2. Evaluate the media center's image. Find out what teachers, students, administrators, and parents think about the services as they are right now.
3. Incorporate changes/suggestions from the evaluation process whenever they are appropriate. It will do more harm than good if you ask for suggestions and then ignore them.

4. Establish a means of regular communications with all staff in your building. If people are electronically connected, a listserv would be useful. The old standby, the newsletter, is still an excellent communications tool.
5. Keep abreast of information concerning television programs, movies, museum exhibits, or other special events that can be tied into the teaching process. This information can be shared through the newsletter, or you may designate a display board in the media center. People will then get accustomed to looking for items and related library sources.
6. Invite teachers to the media center during their planning period. Be available to talk with them and ask if they need any resources. This is also a good time to show off some new acquisition about which they may not know.
7. Develop a cooperative arrangement with the public library or with special and academic libraries. There are times when you will all be able to help one another.
8. Bring in some best-sellers and schedule book review or book discussion sessions with fellow faculty members. There are many people who would love to participate in this type of activity who just do not have time outside of the school day to do so.
9. Enlist help from local bookstores for cooperative projects.
10. Participate in both school and community activities. You can sponsor a club that could use the media center resources, or one that will take you out of your everyday surroundings and show you in a different light. Both approaches have advantages.

SUBCOMMITTEE PROMOTION SCHEDULE FOR SPECIAL EVENTS

The publicity manager's subcommittee oversees the implementation of the promotion schedule to ensure a successful event. The efforts of this subcommittee contribute to the flow and continuity necessary when planning a special event. The guidelines have been developed from experience and from information supplied by media sources. It is best to contact local media outlets to determine their deadlines so that the subcommittee can plan the special event with the media deadlines in mind.

5–12 months prior to event (monthly)	Recruit and meet with committee members Determine audience Project budget Divide tasks (performer contracts, program, logistics)
3–5 months prior	Meet with committee members Talk with sponsors Begin publicity/newsletters Begin audience preparation, book displays, etc.
1–3 months prior	Check on travel arrangements for speaker Meet with committee members Do a walk-through of program Make publicity decisions

Keys to Making Programs Successful

	Invite community leaders
	Assign volunteers
	Send out press materials
2 weeks prior	Arrange for refreshments
	Meet on details with committee
	Continue publicity
	Make reservations for meals
1 week prior	Meet with committee members
	Prepare introductions
	Check on equipment
	Coordinate logistics/refreshments
	Countdown on publicity
	Go through checklists
1 day prior	Arrange as many setups as possible (e.g., microphone, chalkboard, easel, flip-chart, podium)
	Check details with all other committee chairs
Event Day	Oversee setup of room
	Distribute posters
	Open doors to audience
	Introduce presenter
	Oversee refreshments
	Hold program evaluations
	Attend dinner for speaker
1–3 days after	Thank-yous to all volunteers and staff
	Make quick notes on event
	Pay and thank performers
2–4 weeks after	Meet with committee for comment/evaluations
	Compile final report to distribute to all committee members, school principal, and participating sponsors

HINTS FOR MANAGING GREAT SPECIAL EVENTS

One of the essential goals of the school library media program is to contribute to the increased effectiveness of teaching. The following hints will assist the events planner in providing a satisfying educational and social opportunity for those who participate. They should make the experience of planning a special event an enjoyable one for the school library media specialist.

A good events manager makes bringing the event off simple by employing the very best managerial tools. These are some basic ones:

- Identify the objective. For example, is the primary mission of the program to entertain students, or is the goal to build use of the collection?
- Break tasks down into the steps or activities needed to reach that goal. List the areas that will require committee chairpeople.

- Determine a timetable. Work backward from the event date, pinpointing critical dates where a missed deadline would jeopardize the success of the event. Keep this information on a written planning chart.
- Decide on the specific skills needed by chairpeople in each area. Then assign posts or have them select their own committee based on their strengths and weaknesses.
- Delegate authority. It is mind-boggling to be involved actively with every detail. Allow committee chairs to function independently, with the event manager coordinating all efforts.
- Set up a meeting schedule and a reporting process. The event manager must be able to follow up and make sure the committees are completing their tasks.
- And finally, once the event is over, be receptive to criticism and feedback. Each new event will run more smoothly if you have learned your lessons from past programs and events.

Keep in mind the following ongoing management responsibilities:

- Provide information on an ongoing basis, through all media the school uses (examples: newsletters, bulletin boards, intercoms).
- Talk before the PTA and other school supporters.
- Give tours.
- Participate in school and community activities so that people get to know you as a person.
- Write an annual report about the media center, citing achievements and plans for the future. Include instances in which the media center has made a direct impact on the effectiveness of teaching.
- Involve as many others as possible in the planning of special events.

Here are a few additional hints for successful events:

- Choose dates far enough in advance to provide time for arrangements, logistics, and promotion.
- Be explicit in your instructions to performers.
- Have a backup plan. Know what you will do if there is a power outage, a performer who is late or a no-show, a snowstorm.
- Consider a cancellation clause in the contract in the event that you cannot hold the program.
- Prepare your audience in advance. (Example: for an author visit, have your audience read books before the event.)
- Coordinate your efforts with others. Be sure to inform the bookstore, the public library, and any other appropriate townspeople.

8
Programs on a Shoestring: Learning to Budget and Raise Funds for Special Events Programs

One of the most dreaded but necessary aspects of running a special events program is to estimate, develop, and raise the funds that make up the budget. In fact, the amount of money available may very well determine whether the program will be put on by the media center staff or whether professional talent can be hired to do the program.

The yearly planning calendar discussed in Chapter 2 is a helpful tool to use when projecting expenses. It forces you to decide what you want to offer in terms of special events during a given year and provides a visual look at the year as a whole. With the calendar in place, it becomes easier to estimate the amount of funding you will need to carry out your plans and will aid in allocating funds. This process is also helpful in grouping programs together to make a series, especially if they are on similar themes. In addition, it may be helpful if you plan to submit a formal proposal to potential donors.

WHO TO ASK FOR DONATIONS AND IN-KIND SUPPORT

Few of us ever have enough money in our budgets to do everything we want to. However, there are many ways to locate additional funding. In the school system, parents are one of the most enthusiastic groups to approach for financial support, because by supporting special events they directly enrich their children's learning experiences. Parents might be interested in making personal donations. They certainly are very helpful in raising money through bake sales, raffles, and similar traditional fundraisers. However, parents can offer much more than monetary donations. Many have talents, traditions, customs, and skills that they are willing to share with the students. These valuable in-kind donations can really personalize your special events calendar. For example, one parent, who is a cardiologist, talked to the students about the danger of smoking, administered a breathing test to evaluate their lung capacity (the students blew into a disposable mouthpiece that was connected to inhalation equipment), and suggested food substitutions that would increase the nutritional value of their diet. No dollars ever exchanged hands, but this parent made a valuable contribution of his time and knowledge. At the same time, the media center and the classroom teachers were able to tie the program in with the science and health areas of the curriculum. Displays of materials in the media center were also incorporated. All in all, it was a terrific program, presented at no additional cost.

Tapping the business community for funding and for in-kind support is another way for the school library media center to present programs it could otherwise not afford. As noted earlier, businesses have a vested interest in the success of the schools. They want a work force that is prepared to enter the marketplace, and therefore are often eager partners in assisting schools. Some systems have formed formal business partnerships within the district. They may be prompted by the geographic proximity of the business and the school or by other factors. It is important to begin your process of outreach to the business community by first of all checking to see what programs are already in place. A second point to note is that many businesses have community or public affairs representatives whose job it is to find ways for the company to make a positive impact on the community in which it is located. If you want the support of particular businesses, make it a task early on to meet their public affairs personnel. You can do this by calling the company and scheduling an appointment for them to visit the school. Another way of meeting people who make donation decisions for their companies is through networking opportunities. Many local Chamber of Commerce groups have informal breakfast meetings or after work get-togethers that facilitate this process. As a school library media specialist interested in offering special events, it makes sense for you to attend social events of this type. Serving on some community committees that draw their membership from the business population is a way of making your own contribution while meeting people who might be helpful to you in the future. Be sure to have business cards made so that you can exchange cards at events of this kind.

What kinds of donations can you expect from businesses? There is no set rule. They may make an outright cash contribution. They may offer to loan some personnel as volunteer help. The latter can be especially useful, giving you access to talents (graphic, artistic, etc.) that might otherwise not be available or affordable. Some companies may make in-kind donations, in the form of a product or service (for example, a local bakery providing refreshments for parents' night). Each method of contribution will move your project forward, so keep your options open.

Co-sponsorship is another way the school library media center might be able to host special events programs. Civic clubs are another community resource that may be of assistance to the media center. Many clubs have specific giving areas; some even participate in national promotional campaigns that concentrate on specific theme areas (ecology, health awareness, etc). It would be helpful to find people within your school community who are involved in these groups or who have friends or family members who are. They can provide you with the contact names or perhaps make personal introductions that will begin your funding process. If they are not able to assist you, again, check with the Chamber of Commerce or the public library for lists of potential contacts.

Social service organizations are another likely partner. Often they are as financially strapped as school media centers, but by pooling resources, you may be able to finance programs jointly. These agencies also have missions that touch on themes covered in most curricula, so the programming they offer is not only appropriate but helpful in reaching the school's educational objectives.

As noted previously, block bookings with other schools and libraries in your geographic area are another technique for making library media center programs affordable. Block booking simply means that the performer is booked in more than one location in an area in a limited amount of time. This often reduces the price significantly, because it saves the performer travel time and expense. Do not hesitate to ask performers if this is a possibility with them. Very often they are delighted to do block bookings, because they can generate substantial income from them.

HOW TO ASK FOR DONATIONS

Whether you seek cash donations or in-kind support, you must get down to the business of asking. Be prepared to give companies a list of options from which they can select a mode of giving, depending on their size and their commitment to the particular project. Because companies get many requests for donations, it is always best to put your request in writing. Then follow up with a phone call, providing any other pertinent information. Depending on the scope of your request, you may need to include a full proposal. In any event, a cover letter is always in order. The information included in the letter should be concise and to the point. Be sure to draw attention to any unusual or beneficial feature of the program that might entice the company to consider your proposal.

Figures 8.1 and 8.2 are samples that can be adapted for use in tapping the support of the business community. Be sure that your correspondence is neatly typed on official letterhead and that it contains no spelling or typo-

Figure 8.1
Sample Funding Request

Mr. Any Funder
Marine Books
987 Rellim Way
Any Town, R.I. 12345

Dear Mr. Funder:
    The E. Z. Middle School Library Media Center is pleased to announce that Mr. Bob Blue, noted author of *The Blue Sail*, an ocean adventure novel, will be the keynote speaker at the Media Center's Summer Reading Kick-Off Program. He will speak on June 3 at 1 P.M.
    Our goal is to entice our students to keep on reading while they enjoy the sun and surf this summer. With our common interest in books and materials about the sea, we thought that you might like to participate in this program. I will call you the beginning of next week so that we can discuss some possibilities. In the meantime, I hope that you will look over the materials that I am sending along with this letter.
Best regards,

Mary Jo Minor
School Library Media Specialist

Figure 8.2
Sample Proposal

Proposal for Marine Books

Program Sponsor: E. Z. Middle School Media Center

Program Title: Sail into Summer

Date: June 3

Audience: 6th, 7th, and 8th Graders

Program Objective: To encourage students to read while on summer vacation

Program Details: Mr. Bob Blue, noted author, will be speaking at the school. Students will hear how he writes his adventure stories and have a chance to question him. Copies of his book will be available. Booklists of summer reading are being prepared by the Faculty Committee. The program will follow a picnic-style lunch in the cafeteria. Parents/family are invited to attend.

Figure 8.2 (continued)

Possible Sponsorship: Marine Books sets up a table and sells paperback copies of Mr. Blue's books. Mr. Blue will sign the books. Proceeds are split with the Media Center. Marine Books advertises the program in its store. The Media Center puts up a sign thanking Marine Books. Marine Books helps underwrite the cost of the picnic lunch, or provides bookmarks or placemats for all those who attend.

---

graphical errors. Appearance and first impressions are important. They may be the deciding factor in whether or not your proposal gets reviewed.

OTHER SOURCES

There are also organizations with grants available to help various groups promote causes supportive of their mission. *The Foundation Directory* is a good resource for identifying such groups. Many states also produce a directory of foundations within their area. Arts councils and humanities councils also are good contacts to have. Even if they are not able to provide you with direct funding, they may be able to make available a talent bank of individuals who are funded under their umbrella.

Government sources should also be considered. In the past, funding for programs has been available through federal grants. Many states have grants programs, some of which are targeted at specific social problems (gang violence, for example). Be on the lookout for these. Register yourself with various agencies and listservs so that you will be notified when funds become available.

The possibilities for creative programming are endless. Using the talents of many individuals and capitalizing on the creativity and the energy of your own staff will open up a world of programs to your school library media center. One should not limit oneself in the area of special events programs because the money is not there at the outset. Start early, be creative, and the funding will materialize if you believe in your program.

BUDGETING

The budget is one of the most important and effective control devices available to measure library media programs and their effectiveness. A budget sets out the monies that are required over a particular period of time. It includes all of the statistical records (e.g., financial, attendance, age, or demographic statistics) and everything that is of concern for the project. It is a financial plan that works in tandem with your other plans, setting forth both costs and goals. It is used for control, for coordination, for communications, and for performance evaluation.

If the budget is viewed as a part of the evaluation process, it can indicate how successfully goals and objectives have been addressed. Budgeting is a part of the overall planning process, and can be used to demonstrate, to yourself as well as to those who may fund your special events, that the resources obtained have been used effectively and efficiently. Figures 2.13 and 2.14 show sample budgets for special events programs.

9

Resources

All special events require multiple resources, in terms of both people who can help and print and nonprint materials. The good news is that there are numerous sources that can assist you. This chapter provides some practical information to help you locate appropriate speakers and performers. It will also point you in the direction of theme development and help you identify specialized equipment or other materials that will make your special event successful. Note that this is a selected list—there are many other sources that might be useful. If you follow the logic behind this list, however, you will be well on your way to developing the background materials you will need for any special event.

THE CURRICULUM AS A RESOURCE

One of the very best resources that school library media specialists have at their fingertips is the curriculum itself. It makes a great deal of practical sense to develop and arrange special events around the broad topic areas that are already in place. This approach is also likely to be readily acceptable to staff members who may already feel that there is not enough time in a school year to cover all that is expected of them. A further reason for curriculum-based program development is that it can serve as an impetus for increased reading by piquing students' curiosity. The library media specialist must plan ahead and have on hand both print and nonprint resources that will enhance the students' learning. Moreover, varied materials must be available for students to use on an individual basis.

The best thematic programs use interdisciplinary strategies to supplement the curriculum. A good example might be a theater production on

Will Rogers sponsored by the media center. Often done by one actor, this moving monologue makes the history of the period come alive. By incorporating displays and bibliographies of historical novels of the period and appropriate nonfiction and videos, the school library media center can create a memorable special event. The art department might get involved as well by assisting with displays or exhibiting examples of American art.

Other literary genres might also be the impetus behind developing a program theme and would also benefit from a thematic approach. Science can serve as another area. Many museums and aquariums have outreach programs that make school visits possible and can be tied into curriculum lessons. Science fiction could then be used as a follow-up activity, giving a different twist to the original science lesson. Mathematics and architecture is another example of an interdisciplinary program to offer. There are tremendous resources to use in this area.

SOME SPECIFIC EXAMPLES

The athletic departments of many schools are often criticized for overemphasizing sports to the detriment of academics. The school library media center can plan special events programs to help athletic departments overcome this stereotype. And in schools where more effort seems to be put into sports than into reading, programs can draw attention to many well written books for youth on sports figures, both nonfiction and fiction. Movies can also be used. Programs for high school students could stress the importance of teamwork as a management tool in business and industry. School sports promote teamwork and "spirit," positive attitudes that can be transferred to other life situations.

Social issues are another sound resource for program ideas. These issues are discussed as part of the course content, and many young adult novels dovetail conveniently with them, so the literature component is met by the library. One possibility might be to use the book *December Stillness* by Mary Dowing Hahn (1990) as background on the homeless. A special program might include a talk by staff at a homeless shelter or a local soup kitchen. Follow-up projects might include a food collection drive by the students, or a commitment to volunteer at a shelter. This can be especially helpful as more and more school systems are teaching students how to become involved in their community and requiring community service hours to graduate.

Another activity that can tie in with programs of this sort is a lesson on how to keep a journal. A journal becomes a nonthreatening place for students to explore their feelings, to think about things that are happening in the world, and to connect significant events in their life. The value of learning this technique is tremendous. In addition to promoting fluency and language development through writing, journal keeping may also prompt an interest in reading the journals of others. *The Diary of Anne Frank* and Joan Blos' *A Gathering of Days* are two examples of titles that can be used in coordination with a program of this kind.

A related theme might revolve around neighborhoods. In many large urban centers, new emphasis is being placed on the neighborhood. Community policing and neighborhood centers are part of a trend toward breaking down large problems into small, manageable components. Programs of this type might draw from the cultural strengths of the neighborhood. Try starting with the one in which the school is located, and then expanding to other neighborhoods within the city. This can then generate multiple ideas and add true cultural diversity to the program. Items to incorporate as resources would include the folklore as well as the contemporary literary works of a given cultural group; the music, art, crafts, costumes, foods, and traditions of the group can be studied as well. Travel agents are a wonderful resource for this type of program; they are often willing to help as a public relations gesture. The program could culminate with a Parade of Flags, smaller in scope, of course, but similar in spirit to those held at Olympic events, a conclusion apt to draw media attention.

The fine arts area of the curriculum lends itself nicely to promoting and valuing oral language. Thinking, creating, and problem solving are areas of development that are crucial to the fields of art and music. Guests from both professions can be found through local music unions, symphonies, and arts associations. Many individuals from college and university fine arts departments, both professors and students, are willing to put on public performances. Appropriate exhibits could be coordinated by those groups as well. Any number of accompanying activities can be used to round out these programs. Some students may be interested in writing their own musical lyrics. There are even computer programs available to help. Other students might appreciate the opportunity to work in a new artistic medium. Parent volunteers can be of tremendous assistance if a concert or a field trip to a museum is planned as a related activity.

ORGANIZING THEMATIC APPROACHES TO SPECIAL EVENTS PROGRAMS

In order for thematic programs to be successful, it is important to follow a thorough planning process. As always, learning objectives must be clearly established and communicated.

Selection of appropriate thematic programs can be organized by the library media specialist and a steering committee of student grade-level representatives. The viewpoints of all grade members, male and female, can be explored in order to develop specific programs geared to the students' interests, ages, and academic levels. Thematic special events also can be developed to appeal to all age levels so that everyone can participate.

The library media specialist implements learning strategies to challenge, stimulate, and encourage student participation and plans a mixture of activities and pre- and post-event assignments incorporating the special events into the curriculum plan. The library media specialist can also help students select appropriate print and nonprint resources available in the library, to facilitate and aid them in working on assignments derived from the special events.

Sources for Ideas About Thematic Programs

The starting point for thematic programs should be the curriculum unit itself. The various units will automatically provide a list of themes. Seasonal events also lend themselves to thematic treatment. Winter, with its weather changes and the natural adaptations required by plant and animal life, makes a good theme for science special events. The historic remembrance days in January and February tie in well with history and social studies units. Cultural enrichment programs with emphasis on diversity can be appropriate here. Introducing the mystery and suspense genre ties in well with October. Theater productions, storytellers, puppet shows for younger children, and maybe even a participatory murder mystery play for high school students could be held. Chase's Calendar of Annual Events (*Contemporary Books*, annual) is an another useful source for ideas for special events.

BACKUP PROGRAM RESOURCES

In the back of every program planner's mind is the fear that something will go wrong the day of the event. If thorough planning has been undertaken, you will be surprised to see how many problems are really surmountable.

Contingency plans are needed in case of bad weather. Extra equipment and supplies, replacement bulbs, and spare fuses and batteries should be on hand. Unfortunately, there is always the possibility that some last-minute crisis will prevent the performer from appearing. Problems can range from a flat tire to poor health. Professional performers do not take their responsibilities lightly, so the chance of this happening is remote. Good communications, thorough reference checks, and signed contracts help to make such occurrences unlikely. The possibility of facing a last-minute crisis should not deter you from planning special events, but rather make you an even more efficient program planner.

If you have done a good job of promoting an event and expect to have a substantial audience that will be disappointed if there is no program, you had best be prepared to offer an alternative. The wise programmer has an appropriate fill-in activity that can be implemented quickly under emergency circumstances. This might be a videotape or a film (make sure that either has public performance rights) on the same topic, or hands-on activities that can be done in small groups in the classrooms so that they can be adapted by age. In a worst-case scenario, you may have to postpone the performance, rescheduling it for another time. Let's hope this will not happen after all your hard work, but it is best to be prepared.

PRINT RESOURCES FOR SPECIAL EVENTS

American Library Association. *Planning and Role Setting for Public Libraries: A Manual of Options and Procedures.* Chicago: American Library Association, 1987.

America 2000: Library Partnerships. Washington, D.C.: U.S. Department of Education, 1992.

Bonwell, Charles C., and James A. Eison. *Active Learning: Creating Excellence in the Classroom.* Washington, D.C.: U.S. Department of Education, 1991.

Brown, Rexford. *Schools of Thoughts: How the Politics of Literacy Shape Thinking in the Classroom.* San Francisco: Jossey-Bass, 1991.

Burroughs, Lea. *Introducing Children to the Arts: A Practical Guide for Librarians and Educators.* Boston: G. K. Hall, 1988.

Center for the Book. *Book-of-the-Month Club Survey.* Washington, D.C.: Library of Congress, Center for the Book, 1991.

Children's Book Council. *People to Contact to Arrange for Author/Illustrator Appearances.* New York: Children's Book Council, 1994.

Edwards, Margaret Alexander. *The Fair Garden and the Swarm of Beast: The Library and the Young Adult.* Chicago: American Library Association, 1994.

Haycock, Ken. *The School Library Media Program in the Curriculum.* Englewood, Colo.: Libraries Unlimited, 1990.

Hefner, Christine. *Literature-Based Science.* Phoenix, Ariz.: Oryx Press, 1995.

Irving, Jan. *Fanfare: Programs for Classrooms and Libraries.* Englewood, Colo.: Libraries Unlimited, 1990.

Konopka, Gesila. "Requirements for the Healthy Development of Adolescent Youth." *Adolescence* 8 (Fall 1993): 1–26.

Lance, Keith. *The Impact of the School Library Media Center on Academic Achievement.* Castle Rock, Colo.: Hikcow Research and Publishing, 1993.

Leonhardt, Mary. *Parents Who Love Reading, Kids Who Don't.* New York: Crown, 1993.

McElmeel, Sharon. *The ABCs of an Author/Illustrator Visit.* Santa Barbara, Calif.: Lenworth Publishing, 1994.

Polkingham, Anne T., and Catherine Toohey. *More Creative Encounters: Activities to Expand Children's Literature.* Englewood, Colo.: Libraries Unlimited, 1988.

Raines, Shirley C. *Story Stretchers: Activities to Expand Children's Favorite Books.* Mt. Rainier, Md.: Gryphon House, 1989.
Services and Resources for Young Adults in Public Libraries. Washington, D.C.: National Center for Education Statistics, 1988.
Sullivan, Emilie P. *Starting with Books: An Activities Approach to Children's Literature.* Englewood, Colo.: Teacher Idea Press, 1990.
Task Force on Youth Development and Community Programs. *A Matter of Time: Risk and Opportunity in Nonschool Hours.* New York: Carnegie Corporation, 1992.
Vinegard, Sue. *Evaluating Volunteer Programs and Events.* New York: Heritage Arts, 1988.
Weiner, Stephen. *Bring an Author to Your Library.* Fort Atkinson, Wis.: Alleyside Press, 1993.

RESOURCES FOR BUILDING PARTNERSHIPS AND COMMUNITY SUPPORT

As was stated earlier, using partnerships to achieve intended results in special events is an effective strategy. There are many approaches to take, depending on the type of organization you want to join forces with. The following books and organizations provide assistance in this area.

Print Resources

Adams, Don, and Paul Snodgrass. *A Manager's Handbook to Partnerships.* Ellenton, Fla.: Infomedia, 1990.
Childress, Valerie. *Winning Friends for the School Library.* Santa Barbara, Calif.: Lenworth Publishing, 1993.
Hartgul, Gary. *Building Influence for the School Librarian.* Santa Barbara, Calif.: Lenworth Publishing, 1994.
National Association of Partners in Education. *Handbook for Principals and Teachers: A Collaborative Approach for Effective Involvement of Volunteers.* Alexandria, Va.: National Association of Partners in Education, 1994.
Regden, Diana Wyllie. *Bringing Business and Community Resources into Your Classroom: A Handbook for Education.* West Haven, Conn.: National Education Association, 1991.
———. *Business and Schools: A Guide to Effective Programs.* New York: Council for Aid to Education, 1990.
Trotta, Marcia. *Managing Library Outreach Programs.* New York: Neal-Schuman, 1993.
Wekelund, Karen Reed. *Schools and Communities Together: A Guide to Parent Involvement.* Portland, Ore.: Northwest Regional Education Laboratory, 1990.

Organizations

Association of School Business Partnership Directors
P.O. Box 923
Norwalk, Conn. 06852
   This professional association provides a means for educators to network with others who have school partnerships.

Council for Aid to Education
51 Madison Avenue, Suite 2220
New York, N.Y. 10012
   This organization works to have funds contributed by the private sector for education.

National Academy of Sciences
2101 Constitution Avenue NW
Washington, D.C. 20418
   This organization sets the standards for science education.

National Art Education Association
1916 Association Drive
Reston, Va. 22091–1590

National Center for History in the Schools
University of California at Los Angeles
231 Moore Hall
Los Angeles, Calif. 90024
   This project encourages the teaching of history and its integration into the curriculum.

National Council for Geographic Education
1600 M Street NW
Washington, D.C. 20036
   This organization oversees the development of standards for geography.

National Mentor Network
4802 Fifth Avenue
Pittsburgh, Pa. 15213
   This is an organization that encourages networking among volunteers from businesses who serve as mentors.

Volunteer: National Center for Citizen Involvement
1111 No. 19th
Arlington, Va. 22209
   This group encourages the exchange of ideas and information among volunteers.

SOURCES ON PUBLIC RELATIONS AND PROMOTIONS

As noted in Chapter 6, it is vital to make as many personal contacts as possible to assist you with promotional activities for special events. However, if you have not done public relations or promotions before, don't despair! Very often you can get in-kind assistance from advertising professionals. There are also some excellent books to help and companies that offer ready-made promotional materials.

Print Resources

Bueckler, Virginia. *PR for Pennies: Low Cost Public Relations*. Hopewell, N.J.: Sources, 1992.

Canolis, Marion. *The Creative Copycat I and II*. Littleton, Colo.: Libraries Unlimited, 1984.

Cooper, Lee Ann. *Reading Bulletin Books*. New York: The Instructor, 1991.

Edsail, Marian S. *Practical PR for School Library Media Centers*. New York: Neal-Schuman, 1990.

Jones, Linda. *Easy Bulletin Boards for Libraries*. Minneapolis: T. S. Denison, 1989.

Kother, Philip. *Marketing for Non-profit Organizations*. Englewood Cliffs, N.J.: Prentice-Hall, 1990.

Matthews, Judy Gay. *Clipart and Dynamic Designs: For Libraries and Media Centers*. Englewood, Colo.: Libraries Unlimited, 1988.

Thomas, James L. *Motivating Children and Young Adults to Read*. Phoenix, Ariz.: Oryx Press, 1992.

Supply Companies for Promotional Materials

American Library Association
ALA Graphics
Public Information Office
50 East Huron Street
Chicago, Ill. 60611

Children's Book Council
67 Irving Place
New York, N.Y. 10003

Clip Art Company
P.O. Box 722
Monrovia, Calif. 91016

Dover Publications, Inc.
31 E. Md. Street
Mineola, N.Y. 11501

Upstart Library Promotions
P.O. Box 889
Hagerstown, Md. 21741

FUNDRAISING RESOURCES

Corporate Resources

Dermer, Joseph. *The Complete Guide to Corporate Fundraising*. Hartsdale, N.Y.: Public Service Materials Center, 1992.

Renz, Loren, ed. *Corporate Foundation Profiles*. New York: Foundation Center, 1994.

Foundations

Renz, Loren, ed. *The Foundation Directory*. New York: Foundation Center, 1995.

Shellow, Jill R. *Grant Seekers Guide: Funding Sourcebook*. Washington, D.C.: National Network of Grantmakers, 1994.

General

Flanagan, Joan. *The Grass Roots Fundraising Book: How to Raise Money in Your Community*. Chicago: Contemporary Books, 1992.

Seltzer, Michael. *Securing Your Organization's Future: A Complete Guide to Fundraising*. New York: Foundation Center, 1994.

PROFESSIONAL ASSOCIATIONS

Take advantage of opportunities to network with your colleagues on a state, regional, and national level whenever possible. Participate in the continuing education that professional associations offer and be aware of the kinds of events they sponsor. Professional publications and conferences are also good places to learn of resource people who can help with special events, or to locate specialized tests or activities that you might want to duplicate in your school. The following national organizations are among the most useful:

American Association of School Librarians
American Library Association
50 East Huron Street
Chicago, Ill. 60611

Council for Advancement and Support of Education (CASE)
11 Dupont Circle
Washington, D.C. 20036

National Coalition for Parent Involvement in Education
1202 16th Street NW
Washington, D.C. 20036

National PTA
Department D
700 North Rush Street
Chicago, Ill. 60611

MISCELLANEOUS RESOURCES

Barchers, Suzanne, and Patricia Marden. *Cooking Up U.S. History*. Englewood, Colo.: Teacher Idea Press, 1991.

Christenbury, Lelia. *Books for You*. Urbana, Ill.: National Council of Teachers of English, 1995.

Katz, Lillian G. *Helping Others with Teaching*. Urbana, Ill.: ERIC Clearinghouse on Elementary and Early Childhood Education, 1993.

Klasing, Jane P. *Designing and Renovating School Library Media Centers*. Chicago: American Library Association, 1991.

Whitin, David J., and Sandra Wilde. *It's the Story that Counts*. Portsmouth, N.H.: Heinemann, 1995.

Wood, Fred. *How to Organize a School-Based Staff Development Program*. Alexandria, Va., 1993.

Zuchner, Kenneth. *Educating Teachers for Cultural Diversity*. East Lansing, Mich.: National Center for Research on Teacher Learning, 1993.

FINDING APPROPRIATE SPEAKERS AND PERFORMERS

Authors and Illustrators

The marketing departments of publishing companies are the very best resource for locating authors and publishers that participate in special events. Not every able writer is a good speaker! The marketing personnel are very aware of the speaking ability of their authors and will save you the embarrassment of booking a poor speaker. I definitely do not recommend trying to book authors and illustrators directly unless you have an "in" with them.

The amount of time spent and the number of presentations made at your school by an author or illustrator are highly variable. You must ask each and every time; do not assume they will make multiple presentations. Audience size is another variable. Some individuals are very comfortable speaking to overflowing auditoriums; others prefer small group presentations. Again, you must ask each and every time.

Almost all authors and illustrators have set fees, ranging from modest to substantial. In addition, you need to budget for travel, lodging, and meals. On occasion, an author will contribute his/her honorarium to your school, but it is not something that you can count on. You must also remember to ask them if they are interested in doing so.

Literature and Book Discussion Series

Bringing in scholars to discuss literature is another way to appeal to specific groups. Talks can be planned as a series, with the discussion focusing on one author or on a particular genre of literature. This type of program is wonderful to offer to high school students. Targeting teachers and staff or parents is also appropriate.

The best way to locate speaker/scholars for this type of event is through local colleges. Many have speakers' bureaus which feature their faculty. Talks are often offered by colleges for promotional reasons—they want to give their institution public visibility. Often, for this reason, there are no fees for this type of outreach. If any, they are usually modest honoraria.

Arts Councils/Humanities Councils/Museums

Culturally oriented organizations often can put you in contact with various programs, and may have funding sources to assist you as well. Regional or state cultural organizations often receive federal monies earmarked for distribution to local programs, even though federal funding is being cut back in this area. Don't forget to check with local museums and historical societies. These organizations often have a wealth of materials as well as very interested and committed volunteers. A partnership with them is most appropriate. Local history programs are best when they are intergenerational, so that the past remains alive in our young people.

Health and Related Issues

Like museums and colleges, local health providers are very generous in sharing their expertise. Large institutions such as hospitals usually have a community relations liaison who can assist you in finding a speaker or arranging a program on a given topic. An added benefit is that organizations of this kind are eager to reach communities. Their mission is to educate the public. So, nine times out of ten, programs are given at no cost. These organizations also are able to supply additional resource materials, often in the form of giveaways for children.

Music and Entertainment

Performing groups almost always require fees. Fortunately, these are often the easiest fees to have sponsored by an outside organization. In addition, many performers are listed with a musicians' union, which may provide financial subsidies to nonprofit organizations that cannot afford the full fee. These unions are also a valuable source for lists of performers who specialize in specific types of music. The Recording Industry Association of America has an allotment of funds as well.

Travelogues

Travelogues are wonderful to incorporate into a social studies curriculum; all offer tremendous opportunities to showcase cultural diversity. Local travel agencies are a good resource to call on. They may offer to do a program themselves, or they may put you in touch with seasoned travelers who take good slides or videos and are willing to share them with the students. These programs are popular because they describe foreign and exotic places that many students have seen only on a map. The addition of three-dimensional artifacts, crafts, and souvenirs makes these very valuable programs; an added benefit is that often they can be presented for little or no money.

Miscellaneous Resources

- Public Libraries: Check with your public library. Librarians usually keep a list of local people who have programs to offer. They may also have lists of speakers' bureaus and other resources.
- Chamber of Commerce: This organization may have lists of local business people who would be interested in going out and talking to students about how they make or market their product, which is a step beyond career days.
- Clubs and Organizations: In addition to being sources of funding support, some groups exist for purposes that may coincide with your needs. For example, you may locate a group in your community whose purpose is to continue the folk-dancing tradition of Greece. Their purpose and your needs may click.
- Local Newspapers: Find out who the librarian is. Papers often keep files in their "morgue" on people of local fame. Statewide publications would also be very useful for the same reason, but on a broader basis. Read the advertisements as well. It is surprising how many programs can result from these.
- The Yellow Pages: This is a tool that is often overlooked. Remember that it is professionally designed to attract business for the advertisers. This fact is a tremendous help. It really doesn't hurt to pick up the phone and make a few calls. The fact that your program is for children, in schools, is often the best motivation for a business to get involved.

CONCLUSION

As this book makes clear, programs can take many forms and appeal to a variety of ages. They can be stories; they can be demonstrations; they can be performances. Design them to be informative and entertaining at the same time. Taking advantage of the full range of possibilities available can lead to a very well-balanced special events program for your school library media center. A final word—take the time to enjoy it!

Index

Agreements, informal and formal, 51
America 2000, 4, 7
Arts Council, 109
Audience, and planning special events, 6
Author visits, 35, 108–9

Backup plans, 102–3
Benefit analysis, 12, 43, 45
Block bookings, 95
Book discussion series, 109
Book displays, 14, 25, 69
Brainstorming, 19
Broadcast media, 71
Budget, 32, 37, 88–89, 93, 97–98; expenses, 39; income, 40
Business support, 45–46, 94

Chamber of Commerce, as resource, 110
Civic organizations, as resource, 46, 110
Collaboration, 6, 10, 49–50
Commitment letter, 61
Committees, 34–35

Community participation, 49–50, 54
Confirmation letter, 60
Contracts, 86–89; sample, 87–88
Correspondence with provider, 87
Co-sponsorships, 95
Cultural diversity, 7, 85
Curriculum, 5, 11–12, 20–21, 24, 99–102

Donations, 93–95; sample funding request, 96; sample proposal, 96–97

Educational objectives, 10
Educational philosophy, 5, 21
Evaluation, 10, 14, 34, 79–81; sample program evaluation form, 81
Event logistics worksheet, 30, 38
Event scheduler, 33
Events checklist, 63

Families, 5, 25
Financial support, 37, 45, 49
Flyers, 74
Focus groups, 6, 11

Formats, and providing information, 2
Funding of media centers, 4, 37, 52, 94

Goals and goal setting, 4–5

Health providers, as resource, 109
Humanities Council, 109

Ideas, 12, 19–21, 40–41
Illiteracy, combatting, 3
Illustrators, 108–9
Information Power, 1
In-kind donations, 93–94
Interdepartmental relationships, 4, 50
Interdisciplinary enhancements, 5, 20
Inventory, of existing resources, 11

Learning environment, 5
Learning objectives, 83–84
Learning outcomes, 17
Learning styles, 10
Learning theory, 5
Library service, 5
Life skills, 11
Literacy, 5, 13
Logistics, 29–32

Management hints, 91–92
Market segments, 6, 11
Marketing activities, 67
Marketing, external, 8, 11, 69
Marketing, internal, 7, 11, 69
Marketing plan, 7
Marketing strategies, 7
Materials, non-print, 3–4
Materials, print, 2–4, 103–4
Mentoring, 13, 38
Mission statement, 1, 3
Morale, and impact on learning, 13
Museums, as resource, 109

Music and entertainment, as resource, 110

Needs identification process, 6; community analysis, 11; techniques, 11
Newspapers, as resource, 110
Newsletters, 73
Networking, 20

Outreach programs, 50

Parent involvement, 44, 47
Partnerships, 2–3, 43–44, 47, 49–50; with community, 47, 54–55; with parents, 47
Personnel training, 57, 64–65
Planning calendars, 21
Planning process, 4–6, 33, 64
Posters, 69
Principals, role of, 5
Professional associations, 57, 107–8
Professional development, 5, 57
Program overview worksheet, 29, 36
Programs, ideas, 17, 40–41, 100–101; checklist of media types, 85; enhancements, 13; resources, 20–21, 84–85, 99, 102–3, 110
Project information sheet, 52
Promotion, 14, 21, 27, 35, 77, 90, 106–7; schedule, 90
Proposals, 53, 95–97
Press kits, 69; suggested items for, 10
Press releases, 69–71
Public Libraries, as resource, 110
Public relations and publicity, 12, 45, 68, 76, 82, 89–90; analysis worksheet, 68; timing, 77
Public relations plan, 67
Public service announcements, 72

Reading habits, 9, 13
Reading incentives, 12

Index

Reading programs, 13
Reports, 82; sample final report form, 83
Resource-based learning, 2, 10
Resource file, 17
Resource people, 19, 102
Resources, programs. *See* Programs
Risk assessment questionnaire, 31

Sample Media Center Program Calendar, 22, 23; monthly calendar, 75
Sample program ideas, 18
Sample publicity manager's schedule, 77
Sample resource listing, 19
School library media center: goals, 3, 6; role within the school community, 1, 3
School library media specialist, responsibilities, 6, 11
Skills, 33, 57, 79
Special event committee structure, 34

Special events programs, 9; cultural benefits, 10; definition, 9; educational process, 43
Staffing issues, 44
State associations, 27
Student achievement, 7; as participants and partners, 49

Teamwork, 13
Themes, 9–10, 40–41, 99–101; sources, 101–2
Travelogues, 110
Training, 61–63; event coordinator's training checklist, 63

User groups, 6

Volunteer rercruitment form, 59
Volunteer training checklist, 62
Volunteers, 57–61, 64–65

Whole learning, 4

Yellow pages, as resource, 110

About the Author

MARCIA TROTTA is executive director of the Meriden, Connecticut, Public Library and adjunct professor of Library and Information Science at Southern Connecticut State University. She has developed many special events programs in her library that have earned her local and state recognition, including the Outstanding Librarian Award from the Connecticut Library Association in 1986 and again in 1993. She is a past president of the Connecticut Library Association and serves on the Connecticut State Library Board of Directors.